R E A D I N G
THE HORSE'S
M · I · N · D

Jackie Budd

HOWELL
BOOK HOUSE

NEW YORK

HOWELL BOOK HOUSE
A Simon & Schuster / Macmillan Company
1633 Broadway
New York, NY 10019

MACMILLAN is a registered trademark of Macmillan, Inc.

Library of Congress Cataloging-in-Publication data

Budd, Jackie
    Reading the horse's mind / Jackie Budd. 1st U.S. ed.

            p.   cm.
    ISBN 0–87605–744–X
        1. Horses – Behaviour.   2. Horses – Psychology   3. Horses – Training
    I. Title
    SF281.B84   1996
    636.1'008'8 — dc20   96–17636
                                                                     CIP

Printed and bound in Singapore by Kyodo Printing Co.

10 9 8 7 6 5 4 3 2

● ● ● ● ● ● ● ● ● ● ● ● ● ● ● ● ● ●

This book is dedicated to my Mum and to my Dad, who could never quite understand what this fascination with horses was all about, but still tolerated my curious obsession.

● ● ● ● ● ● ● ● ● ● ● ● ● ● ● ● ● ●

CONTENTS

ACKNOWLEDGEMENTS

I would like to thank all the experts who so willingly squeezed time for yet more 'horse talk' into their busy schedules: the Balance Team, David Broome CBE, Stephen Hadley, Carl Hester, Susie Hutchison, Mary King, Sylvia Loch, Richard Maxwell, Karen O'Connor, Gillian O'Donnell, Marcy Pavord, Monty Roberts, Linda Tellington-Jones, and Lesley Ward for her contributions from the United States of America and particularly for the interview with Susie Hutchison.

Special thanks to Nick for his support, to Julia Menzies and to all those who helped with supervision of my own little 'animals', especially my folks and Sharon Evans.

Thanks to EMAP Pursuit Publishing for use of photographs, unless otherwise credited.

*I*NTRODUCTION

What is this animal, the horse? What is he thinking about as he subjects a newcomer to serious scrutiny amidst much snorting and squealing, when he rolls his eye with suspicion and jumps in the air at a friendly pat on the quarters? Yet, this is the same animal who can gallop fearlessly towards a blind drop at Badminton, or will dance down the centre line in a Grand Prix dressage test, just daring the audience not to admire him.

Business or friendship, we would never expect to strike up an effective partnership with another person if we knew next to nothing about who they really were, where they came from, what motivated them and what their aims were in life – and that is talking about the same species! The way that a horse thinks and reacts is the basis of everything that he does. Yet how many riders – novices and experts alike – have ever stopped to consider, in any depth, what kind of creature they are handling, sitting on and making ever more exacting physical

When a communication exists between rider and horse, great partnerships have been forged.

and psychological demands of?

The horse, our companion over thousands of years of history, seems to be suffering from a case of 'familiarity breeds contempt'. He has been around so long, doing our bidding and sharing our lives in one way or another, he tends to be taken for granted – like a pair of well-worn boots that are used, then polished and put away until next time. In reality though, we have hardly begun to get to know this 'old friend' at all.

The growth of riding for pleasure and sport has given us an opportunity to put our relationship on a new footing. There is no longer a need to exploit the horse's strength and good nature for the sake of our own survival. Now we can stand back and look at what we have. At last we have time to find out a bit more about our collaborator, and, in understanding him, we can offer him a better deal. This new relationship should stem from affection, but it should also come from a sense of fair play and respect.

To go forward we need to step back and start again, almost from scratch. We need to see the horse first and foremost as an animal with its own unique qualities, we must find out what makes a horse tick, and how he learns and understands. When the communication is there, great partnerships have been forged – illustrated by many of the horsemen and women interviewed in this book. Yet communication and understanding should not be a lottery. For every horse and rider that share the same wavelength, there are all too many frustrated riders and unhappy, misunderstood horses that never come close. If we can appreciate how nature made the horse, we can work with the shaping of millions of years of instinct and evolution, instead of against it. This book is aimed at helping owners and riders to get to know their horses, to learn from them and to set up some real lines of communication. In this way, we can come a little closer to understanding the nature of the horse, and what it is reasonable to ask of him.

1 EVOLUTION OF THE HORSE

IN THE BEGINNING

The story of life on the Earth is a long one, stretching ever longer as scientists push its beginnings further and further back in time. Barely two centuries ago it was widely believed that the planet itself was a mere 6,000 years old, with the starting post for plant and animal life positioned just a matter of days later. By the 19th century the study of geology had shown how way out of line that reckoning was – an estimate of hundreds of millions of years was closer to the mark. We now know that the figure is nearer a mind-numbing 4.5 billion years. The passage of time on this kind of scale is, like astronomers' light-years, almost impossible to imagine without giving some reference points to work with. One of the easiest and most frequently used comparisons is to see the age of the Earth as a single day. Starting at midnight, we would have to wait eight hours before encountering the primitive life-forms that produced the earliest fossils, some 3000 million years ago. Morning, afternoon and most of the evening would pass before dinosaurs appear on the scene at about 10.40pm. The first modern humans make their entrance even later, clocking in with less than a couple of minutes to go before midnight strikes again. The few seconds-worth of human civilisation allowed by our time-clock illustrates what newcomers we really are.

So where does the horse fit into the scheme of things? The distant ancestors of the horse were among the Earth's oldest mammals, with a lineage reaching back long before the first whales appeared and many millions of years before the first monkeys, never mind men. As he began to straighten up and take his first faltering steps on two legs, the earliest hominid would have shared his world with a horse-like creature whose physical appearance and patterns of behaviour we could easily recognise today. By the time modern humans were beginning to make any kind of mark on their surroundings, the horse had already undergone 50 million years of design improvement that had transformed him from a diminutive forest scamperer to a large grassland galloper.

Evolution is a painstakingly gradual process. For almost as long as the dinosaurs themselves, the mammals had been a successful group – artful dodgers scuttling between the huge, clawed feet of their gargantuan cousins. The demise of the great reptiles, however, left mammals victors by default, clearing the field for these tiny jacks-of-all-trades to grow in stature and come into their own. By the close of the

Cretaceous period some 65 million years ago, most of the key features of the mammals' winning formula were well established. These included: teeth that were precisely adapted to specialised food processing; the progression away from egg laying to carrying young; sophisticated sensory mechanisms and an increasingly efficient nervous system.

It was the agility and flexibility of these little generalists that probably enabled them to survive the catastrophic environmental lurch that wiped out the dinosaurs, whose size, weight and slowness to adapt proved their undoing. Now the mammals flourished, migrating in all directions across the land bridges that joined the continents, slowly specialising into running, climbing, digging or swimming experts as conditions required. There are no guarantees in the game of survival, however. It has never been a foregone conclusion that any one particular plant and animal species will survive and automatically 'learn' to cope better with their new circumstances and then gradually adapt to them. Evolution is a lottery in which the stakes are high.

THE PROCESS OF SELECTION

The description of the evolutionary process as the 'survival of the fittest' is a misleading one because 'bad luck' plays as big a role as 'bad genes'. As our knowledge of paleontology has grown, it has become obvious that no form of life has reached the present day by a smooth and effortless progression, by repeatedly out-performing creatures less 'fit' than itself. Fossil records show how, time and time again, sheer force of circumstance had the greatest impact on the path life took. Countless species continued – as they do today, frequently helped along by humankind – to fall by the wayside as their food supplies ran out, their habitat was destroyed or a natural disaster wiped them out. Many strains of horse ancestor were among those which did not make it. Who knows what kind of horse we might have had today if other conditions had prevailed and preserved the three-toed forest dwellers of the Miocene period?

As the rules of existence were repeatedly thrown up in the air and fell to the ground, species that came through each upheaval found that they were forever up against a different game plan. The 'fittest' were those best suited to the new order of play. All species which have managed to survive through to the present day deserve admiration for being very talented players, having successfully ridden out this game of evolutionary Russian roulette for many millions of years. The process of natural selection, which determines which animals will thrive and which will die out, works entirely by chance. Genes, sets of chemicals within our body cells that carry the information determining individual characteristics, are inherited by an individual on pairs of chromosomes. One of each pair is received from the mother and one from the father. Some characteristics are dominant, and some recessive, so no individual is ever an exact replica of its parents. In addition, genes are constantly and randomly throwing up changes or

'Evolutionary change is not restricted to physical adaptations...it applies equally to behaviour'

'mutations' which result in further slight differentiation between individuals within a species.

When a difference results in the animal being better adapted to a particular environment at a particular time, that individual will live longer and therefore produce more offspring, all likely to inherit that advantageous gene, which then becomes more frequent in the population. The strengths or 'fitness' of an animal, lie in the features they possess which 'fit' them to their environment and give them the edge in the survival stakes, enabling them to use their surroundings most effectively, and to pass on that ability too. This constant invention of fresh mutations and strategies keeps up the selective pressure, increasing the odds for the survival of at least some individuals, which then provide the blueprint of a new design. The winners and losers are dictated by the nature of the change of circumstances, not by any inherent superiority in that individual's differences.

Evolutionary change is not restricted to physical adaptations but applies equally well to behaviour too, a great deal of which is inherited through genes. Behaviour patterns that keep an animal alive most effectively would be passed on to more offspring. Each individual is driven in everything that it does – whether it be feeding, playing or socialising – by what will maximise its own survival chances. This applies equally to any offspring, who will carry a set of the crucial family genes on to future generations. Social patterns develop within a group because of a kind of

> *'Each individual is driven by what will maximise its own survival chances'*

unwritten agreement between all parties that this is the best strategy for increasing every individual's survival odds.

ANCESTORS OF THE HORSE

We are lucky in that the horse's evolution follows a classic trail, well-documented by a mosaic of fossil evidence which, although far from complete, gives us quite an accurate picture of development from primeval times.

The oldest complete skeleton discernible as an ancestor of the horse was discovered embedded in rocks in the United States in 1867. It was later found to be genetically identical to skull bones unearthed in southern England some years before. It could be dated at some 50 million-plus years old. Hyracotherium, originally named Eohippus or the 'Dawn Horse' by the American scientists, came from the Eocene period. At this time the Atlantic Ocean was still a marshy swamp and swathes of tropical rainforest covered most of the earth, linking North America with what is now Europe and Asia.

These animals bore a much greater resemblance to the shrew-like mammals of the dinosaur age than anything equine we know today. Hyracotherium would have weighed an average of about 5.5 kg (about 14 pounds) and ranged between heights of 25 and 50 cms (between10 and 20 inches), making it much the size and shape of a fox or a collie-type dog. Its small, low-crowned teeth with slight ridging on the faces of the molars were suited to browsing and nibbling at succulent young leaves, buds and berries – a pastime that most of our own horses still enjoy when given the choice between a tasty young-leafed hedge and their pasture! Predators could be best avoided by a rapid scuttle into the camouflage of the surrounding foliage, so lateral vision was not yet necessary. Eyes were positioned towards the front of the head, more like our own. Most significantly, Hyracotherium supported its four-toed forefeet and three-toed hind feet, tipped by thick horny 'hoofs', with pads like those belonging to dogs and to tapirs, the closest relatives of today's horses. These pads were effective in preventing it from sinking into the soft, wet ground.

Hyracotherium was doing quite nicely until climatic cooling began to be reflected in his environment. Alterations in the distribution of rainfall resulted in trees spreading out to enable more water to be absorbed during the dry season. There were no grassy plains as yet, but the forest floor opened up, encouraging low shrubby vegetation. This, in turn, could feed a larger population of ground-dwelling species, enabling them to develop in size and speed of movement. Some hyracotheria must have carried a mutated gene, giving them slightly harder, longer teeth which were better able to chop and grind the tougher vegetation generated by the cooler, drier conditions. A longer jaw could make way for these teeth, and a slightly lengthened neck would allow the animal easier access to the ground vegetation. Many mammals best suited to tropical conditions faced extinction during the rapid cooling of the Oligocene period, from around 40 to 30 million years ago. As the typical Eocene habitat diminished, cut off from migration routes, those which could not adapt did not survive. Exploiting the mixed woodland that now covered almost all of the world's temperate regions came the gazelle-sized Mesohippus. Mesohippus was still a browser rather than a grazing animal.

However, his low-crowned teeth, and the ridges on the tables of his molars, resulted in a powerful and efficient chopping action, capable of processing the variety of leaf textures that a deciduous woodland would provide throughout the year. The other significant change was in the lower limbs, as Mesohippus developed longer legs and abandoned the fourth toe on the forefeet. Even so, the feet pads remained, showing that a springy base was still useful for moving around the soft soil and scrub of the Oligocene period. Then as the wheel of evolutionary fortune continued to turn, these woodland specialists found themselves at a disadvantage. The climate continued to dry and cool, and as plains of tough, wiry grasses with few trees replaced the woodlands, several different strains of horse ancestor managed to come up with the necessary adaptations. From here on the full story becomes a complicated network of overlapping types ranging freely between North America, Europe and Africa. Most tenacious of the survivors was "merychippus", generally considered to be the true progenitor of the modern horse family.

PLAINS DWELLER

Those animals that continued producing feet with multiple digits and pads, and teeth designed for leaf-nibbling soon found themselves struggling on the dry and open Miocene savanna. Plains-dwellers were exposed and vulnerable to an ever-increasing numbers of carnivorous predators – all opportunists adapting equally fast to their changing surroundings. Self-protection was rapidly becoming a top priority. Before the last Ice Age, Mesohippus had already established two of the fundamental characteristics of the modern horse – his eating tools and his escape mechanism. By the Pliocene period, some five million years ago, all the different lineages descended from the merychippus stock were extinct bar three. Hipparion, with his three toes intact, had migrated west through Eurasia into Africa. The leggy Pliohippus, living on the North American prairies, was now around 120 cms (47 inches) high and had dispensed with the vestiges of his side-toes to rely on a single hoof. One other line had also stumbled across this highly successful innovation – Equus. What it was that eventually gave Equus the edge over these other groups remains a mystery of evolution. However, by the end of the Pleistocene age, around one million years ago, he was the sole survivor. The others had disappeared, overtaken by the rapid spread of Equus to all corners of the Old and New Worlds.

A more wholesale success story is hard to imagine. Supremely adapted to the demands of his habitat and way of life, Equus' takeover was complete. His key features present a very familiar picture:

TEETH: Now highly-crowned and extremely strong, coated in protective enamel and filled with cement. Well-lophed (ridged on the tables), essential for the grinding action required to shred up a fibrous diet of harsh grasses. The tearing canine teeth recede, leaving incisors for chopping, and a large and powerful jaw full of molars. As the tooth wears down with constant use, unworn portions are pushed up from inside the jaw.

HEAD: An open prairie dweller would be short-lived if his source of food obscured his vision. Besides accommodating his many teeth, the long head also keeps the eyes well clear of grass level.

EYES: Positioned near the sides of the head, giving almost all-round vision. Highly sensitive to movement.

EARS: Extremely mobile. Set high and concave in shape in order to pick up maximum range and quantity of sound. The inner ear is protected from damage by a lining of hair.

NOSE AND LIPS: Extremely sensitive at distinguishing different herbage which is crucial when the length of the nose and the eye position prevent the area immediately under the mouth and nose being seen.

NECK: Needs to be long and strong, but flexible enough to aid low feeding and aid vision at ground level and when raised.

HEART AND LUNGS: Large and efficient, housed in a deep and spacious thoracic cavity.

ABDOMEN: Large, to deal with continuous stream of fibrous material that takes a great deal of breaking down, processing and digesting.

LEGS: All-round skills have been sacrificed for specialised running ability. The forearm and lower leg have lost the flexible 'swivel' design of more generalist mammals, opting instead for stability and strength. Reduction of the ridged 'spine' on the scapula (shoulder blade) shows muscles needed to lift the forearm up and outwards are less important than channelling energy into a powerful forward-back thrust. Folded angles between the shoulder and elbow allow huge scope for extension to create a ground-covering action. With little twisting or rotation required, the ulna is reduced leaving a long, strong radius. The knee, which equates to our own wrist joint, is relatively constricted and the long bones of what would be the hand are lengthened and reduced to one strong cannon bone.

Unlike our spread hand, the equine's digits are compressed to just one: the horse becomes an "unguligrade", moving on the tip of a single finger – his hoof. Fully occupied with carrying the body's weight, the digit loses its usefulness for other purposes such as manipulating and scratching – one very good reason for helping your horse out with a few of the things he cannot do for himself, like a nice rub behind the ears!

The length of the leg is obviously important to raise the animal well above the grass, so movement is unimpeded. Heavy muscling is concentrated at the top to drive the stride, but motion is focused in the lightweight lower limb, keeping energy expenditure to a minimum. What was once the foot pad has become a useful spongey anti-slip and anti-concussion fitting – the frog.

SKIN: Highly sensitive, with reflex twitching muscles useful for fly removal, becoming more important with reduced flexibility of the legs. Coat hair can adapt to seasonal weather conditions by thickening or thinning. Plenty of mane and tail hair provide extra insulation and are also useful fly-whisking tools.

A full picture of behaviour cannot be deduced from fossil evidence, though where physical characteristics point to heightened sensory awareness and a power-packed

means of escape, the ground-plan is clear enough. With the mechanics so perfectly tuned to survival, it's reasonable to assume that Equus' behaviour patterns had also had their part to play in the success story and, by the end of the last Ice Age, were likely to have been equally well established – and recognisable to us. Around ten thousand years ago these horses roamed Europe and Asia, eventually cut off from the American continent as the seas rose. Migration to and from the Old and New Worlds had previously been uninterrupted, but for some reason that science still has not been able to explain fully, lack of fossil evidence shows us that equines died out in North America around this time. The horse did not set hoof again on the land of its birth until the sixteenth century brought the Spanish conquistadores to its shores.

THE DOMESTIC HORSE

Theories about how Equus crystallised into the foundation stock of the domestic horse abound, with much confusing disagreement about groups, sub-groups and their labelling. What can be agreed upon is that by the time man first took notice of these fleet-footed beasts sharing his homelands, the on-going process of evolutionary change had produced a huge variety of fine-tuning within the genus Equidae.

Again it was climate, linked with the period of original migration, which provided the catalyst for diversification. The most primitive types arrived when conditions were still warm and tropical. As the climate cooled they stayed in the more hospitable

'The most primitive types arrived when the climate was still warm and tropical'

RIGHT: No longer primarily a browser, equus caballus is still partial to a tasty piece of hedgerow or a leafy branch.

BELOW: The common zebra, with numbers of around 500,000 mainly spread across Kenya and east Africa, is the only one of four surviving zebra species not under threat of extinction.

regions of Africa and the Middle East to become the zebras and asses. All, except the common zebra, are sadly very low in numbers now and some, such as the eastern asses, are barely clinging to survival – victims of either their intractability or their inflexibility, and therefore their limited usefulness to man in comparison with their versatile, equable and athletic cousin, equus caballus.

Another near relative to have experienced a close brush with extinction is equus Przewalsksii Poliakov, or the Asiatic Wild Horse. Differentiated from modern domestic breeds by its chromosome count of 33 pairs (as opposed to the usual 32 pairs), a small herd of the Przewalski's Horse was re-discovered by the Polish explorer whose name it bears, during an expedition to the remote Mongolian steppes in 1881. The world's last truly wild horse finally succumbed to captivity, but after a successful breeding programme is now being carefully reintroduced into its original homelands.

Though technically a distinct species, the Asiatic Wild Horse can be crossed with domestic horses to produce fertile hybrids, so it must be very closely related. Some experts believe it to have been the pro-genitor of all modern breeds, while others consider it more likely to be a member of the primeval pony sub-group of the northern horse (see below). The Przewalski's primitive features would certainly have made him familiar to the prehistoric artists who depicted their quarry on the walls of the caves of Lascaux in southern France.

But it was Equus Caballus who became the hero of the Equidae. Right across the Northern Hemisphere from Morocco to Mongolia, working on the basic framework that had served equus so well, these horses

developed specialised features geared to their local habitats. Broadly speaking, by the time of the earliest domestication, various general types had evolved which, between them, are thought to have made up the stock on which modern breeds and types were founded:–

THE SOUTHERN GROUP is the basis of today's 'hot-blood' breeds, originating from early migrants who moved south to stay in arid regions. They were lean and leggy, with dense bone and small, hard feet. Heat loss was facilitated by thin skin, a fine coat and a high-set tail. The tapered head and expansive nostrils help to filter dry, dusty hair. Sub-types resulted in modern breeds such as the rangy Akhel-Teke, the Caspian pony and the Arab.

THE NORTHERN GROUP became the basis of today's 'cold-blood' breeds. Migrating later, it was already adapting to cooler conditions and stayed further north, closer to the advancing ice where vegetation was lusher. Sub-types that developed included the bulky tundra or Forest horse, the probable ancestor of today's European draught breeds, and the small, mobile and resilient primeval ponies who spread far and wide into the remotest regions, coping with the harshest of environments and poorest pastures, so remaining small. The closest modern relative to these ancient toughies would be the Exmoor – the only surviving breed to retain the jaw formation of prehistoric fossils recently discovered in Alaska.

Both pony and giant northern types feature thick skins and dense coats and heavily-feathered legs, effective insulation against cold and rain. Round bodies, short legs and wedge-shaped necks all minimise

ABOVE: Przewalski's Horse is a separate species of equus with many unique and primitive features. As Przewalskis can be crossed with domestic horses to produce fertile offspring, the two species must be very closely related.

BELOW: Hot-bloods such as the Arab, are thought to have developed from a Southern horse group already making adaptations to life in a hot, dry environment.

loss of body heat. The coarse convex-nosed head of the tundra horse allowed freezing air to be warmed. An extra lumbar vertebra gave more space for the digestive organs. With few natural predators, neither physical nor mental agility were priorities. Huge, broad feet helped spread the horse's weight on boggy terrain and strong pulling muscles on the forehand aided movement out of soft ground more effectively than propelling muscles in the quarters.

One further line does not fit neatly into this picture and has been given a separate species classification – the Tarpan. The genuine wild Tarpan had been hunted to extinction both in the Ukranian steppes and the east and central European forests by the last century. Recently this ancient pony has been 'reconstructed' in captivity in Poland in an attempt to retain its distinctively primitive features. Opinion now inclines towards classing the Tarpan as the product of early crossing between the southern proto-Arab type horses and northern pony types.

FIRST HUMAN CONTACT

For hundreds of thousands of years, contact between the horse and mankind was limited to glimpses of each other from a distance, neither having an inkling of how closely their futures would become entwined. Stone Age man was primarily a cave-dweller or nomad, a hunter-gatherer whose diet consisted mainly of plant material, fruit and leaves. Meat provided a welcome feast when available, but we were far from the full-time killers we were to become.

Prehistoric cave paintings and bone remains show that men appreciated that these stocky, muscle-packed beasts could feed a family for weeks, but effective pursuit of such fleet-footed and reactive animals was

a hopeless waste of energy. So, early on, he probably relied upon scavenging the carcasses of horses killed by other predators, or more dramatically, stampeding a herd of horses off a cliff-edge or into a blind ravine, where many would be trampled to death in the ensuing panic. As man's intelligence, organisational skills and weapon-making skills increased, humans became the hunters and horses the hunted.

The prey still held the upper hand, so at

The Northern group eventually produced equus 'supreme opportunist' – the Primeval Pony – and the huge, and slow-reacting cold-bloods which were to become the mainstay of agricultural development in Europe's heavy soils.

20

first it was the slow, the weak and the young from passing herds who were hijacked, trapped, or picked off by spears and eaten. The human threat, however, still paled into insignificance beside that of more stealthy and athletic carnivores such as the leopard, or indeed, the old enemy – climatic change.

It is ironic, when man's interference in the animal kingdom so often condemns species to the sidelines or to an early exit from evolution, that in the case of the horse he may in fact have come to the rescue. Evidence suggests that by the end of the Ice Age wild horse numbers were slowly but surely falling, not due to predation but as a consequence of encroachment of forest and woodland across the grassy plains that had made up all the temperate zones of the earth. With environmental change taking place more rapidly than natural selection could adapt them to it, eventual extinction could have been staring the savanna specialists in the face. A chance for survival lay just around the corner, though the price was a costly one – their freedom.

By this time early humans has realised that by catching and enclosing a few of these horses they could guarantee a ready supply not only of fresh meat but also of nutritious milk, tough hide, wiry hair, and long strong bones for weapons and tools. Sheep, goats, and later, cattle, had long since become candidates for domestication, and now attention was turned to the horse. Man still led an essentially travelling lifestyle focused on one continual search for fresh food supplies for his animals and himself, probably following the routes of the wild herds as he went. The breakthrough came

when it was decided to put the captured horses to use on these long and difficult migrations.

Strapping a heavy burden of some kind, even a sick or injured person, to the back of a well-tamed ass (the earliest draught equines were onagers, known to have been in use some 3000 years ago) or horse was probably the first time equines were allocated a new role as labour-saving helpmates rather than meal tickets. As beasts of burden, carrying loads, then later dragging them, horses opened up distant horizons to peoples whose range of movement had always been dictated by the weakest members of the tribe.

Climatic warming and the melting of the ice caps now produced an increase in soil fertility and spread of vegetation that hastened man's transformation from a forager to a farmer. Gradually it became practical and profitable to settle in one place rather than to be constantly on the move.

'With the rise of man came the rise of the tame horse ...and the decline of his wild forbears'

Pockets of primitive hunter-gathering and nomadic ways of life remain to this day, but it was the development of agriculture that paved the way for the rapid spread of civilisation throughout most regions of the world. Inextricably linked with the rise of man came the rise of the "tame" horse – and the decline of his wild forebears.

By the second millennium BC this relative newcomer to the domestic scene was turning the tide, increasing in numbers and spreading in all directions. It is not difficult to see why. The impact of the horse on human progress was nothing short of a bombshell.

THE BIRTH OF CIVILISATION

The pasture that fed the tribe's livestock and increased its wealth and standing was a precious commodity, which men were prepared to fight for. Horses – at first harnessed to the chariot and later ridden – turned herdsmen into warriors and raiders for whom distance was no object. By 2000 BC written and pictorial evidence begins to mount up from sources as widely spread as ancient Egypt, Mesopotamia and China, showing horses in elaborate harness, pulling chariots of soldiers and kings, asses laden under the weight of goods and possessions, horses carrying soldiers armed with spears, bows and arrows. Horse peoples swept across the steppes of Euro-Asia into western Europe, ancient Persia and what is now the Middle East, opening up highways for trade and the cross-fertilisation of ideas and social structures.

With the notable exception of the great civilisations of South America, settlements where there were no horses made little gain on a very primitive way of life. The case of the Plains Indians of the Americas illustrates how an established society was transformed by the opportunity to hunt, travel and defend itself from horseback. Those advanced horse cultures that learnt to utilise the horse's versatility fully, such as the Hittites, Mesopotamians, Egyptians and eventually the Greeks and Romans, built powerful and far-flung empires on its back.

UTILISING THE HORSE

The horse provided the sinews of power as it has continued to do throughout human history right up until times of living memory. Cavalry, in various shapes and forms and with ever-more deadly weaponry, dictated the pace of war for three thousand years. Nothing could be a more pointed indication of the horse's extraordinary courage and willingness to co-operate than the horrendous sacrifices made throughout the history of warfare, in the thick of the worst pain and panic that men of each successive age could devise, by such a nervous creature whose every instinct tells it to flee.

Though war was the primary function of the horse right up until the 19th century, society was equally dependent on equine muscle and pace in many other more peaceful ways. The invention of the wheel coupled with the harnessing of horse-power got society on the move. In northern Europe, pack and riding horses predominated until improvement of roads and carriage design led to the heyday of horse transportation from the late 1600s to mid-1800s. It is estimated that in London in the 1890s the bus, railways and hackney carriages alone accounted for an inner-city population of some 50,000 horses. Every conceivable vehicle was horse-drawn, from an elegant private carriage to taxi cab, public trolley bus, brewer's dray and refuse cart. A city horse's working life was hard and short. Few owners had time for the 'sentimentality' of Anna Sewell's *Black Beauty*. The use of the horse in the cultivation of land came late. Where horses had helped create civilisations and mobilise armies, they were valued far too highly to be considered for such menial tasks, which could readily be undertaken by oxen, asses and mules. However, by the Middle Ages when harness was sufficiently developed to bear heavy loads and bigger horses were being bred for warfare, horses became part of the agricultural labour force. By the 18th and 19th centuries, as farming practices and implements adapted to meet the needs of exploding populations, the greater pulling power and versatility of the

Horses were still making the ultimate sacrifice for man as recently as the Second World War. 'Horse Artillery' by Ludwig Macaig.

heavy draught horse led to a golden age of horse-power. At the plough, on the canal tow-path, strapped to the ginwheel, horses laid the foundations for the Industrial Revolution which was eventually to liberate him from the harshest of his labours.

The history of man's use of the domesticated horse was never all work and no play. His thirst for competition pitted horse against horse, whether harnessed to a chariot or with a man astride, from very earliest times. A form of the game of polo is known to have been played in Persia in the sixth century BC. Hunting for sport was a privilege of the kings and nobles of every society from ancient times. It was the increasing enclosure of land that required greater galloping speed and the fostering of

a hitherto little-used equine ability – his jump. This sowed the seeds for a future for the horse after machinery took over, one by one, almost all of his traditional tasks.

It all appears heavily one-sided, this whistle-stop overview of man's exploitation of the horse from the time our paths first crossed right up until the present day. Despite the shameful abuse with which the history of our association is littered, human contact has not been all bad news for the horse. Domestication did in all probability save his skin, and, through the improvement of his environment and selective breeding, has allowed the horse's adaptability to keep pace with human progress at a speed natural selection could never have maintained. Instead of being used and

By the end of the 18th an 19th centuries, the heavy draught horse reigned supreme on the farm. This was the golden age of horse power.

Down the mines, on the roads, and along the canal tow-paths – equine muscle powered the Industrial Revolution.

agriculturalists remained largely within their own region, their tamed livestock thrived in their own milieu and individual animals remained much the same as each other in body and behaviour.

Selective breeding took place in a crude form from the very dawn of domestication, as men chose the horses that were easiest to handle to mate with others of the same tractable character, the stockily-built with the stockily-built in the hope of creating another equally strong pack animal, and so on. Without a clue about the workings of genetics, man knew that matching like with like increased the chances of producing offspring with similar qualities to the parents, but restricted mobility meant that as yet there were little fundamental changes.

discarded, by fitting in with our demands so readily, the horse was saved from falling fatally by the side of the road as man marched on without a backward glance.

THE CREATION OF BREEDS

It was recently estimated that today there exist somewhere in the region of 200 distinct breeds of horse or pony under the species heading Equus Caballus. This impressive total illustrates how rich and varied the equine world has become, largely artificially created by man to suit his own purposes. It was not always that way, as we have seen. Before humans decided to step in and intervene in the natural order of things, wild horses had adapted themselves extremely effectively to local conditions. While early

The Thoroughbred: A truly man-made creation, designed purely for racing.

Then movement and trade in horses began to mix the gene pool. Wild horse types from one area were mated with those from another, adapted to different local conditions. Where there was planning, the aim, as ever, was to produce offspring featuring the best of both the parents. In those days selective breeding was something of a hit and miss affair (and many would say it still is!). The resulting crosses might suit their new environment well, or might struggle without extra attention and care. They might be ideally suited to the work that their breeder had in mind, or be a total disappointment, especially if radically different types were mated, diluting each other's strongest traits. However, by trial and error over many hundreds of years, the consistency of peoples' requirements eventually resulted in regional 'breeds' sharing common characteristics. Though well-matched to the work needs, ways of life and environmental conditions of the locality, all kept the blueprint features of their wild ancestors very much intact.

Inter-breeding was so indiscriminate at first that the original sub-types of true, wild horse were soon completely obliterated. Mixing went on to such a degree that, even as breeds became established, there was huge variation between the looks of individuals. There was no guarantee that any particular pair of parents would breed 'true to type' with no genetic throw-backs. This gambling element remains one of the fascinations of breeding to this day and holds true for the majority of breeds, even where a stud book has been closed to new blood for some time and the gene base is relatively narrow – as in the case of the Thoroughbred.

There was a further influence on the changing appearance of the horse. Men came to realise that the odds on stock growing large and strong could be increased, and working capacity much improved, by supplementing a natural diet of grass with produce from his increasingly efficient efforts at agriculture. Feeding grain throughout the horse's life could offset the weakening effect of transferring a less hardy breed outside the region to which it was best adapted. Yet more options for breeding and use were opened up. Now it was possible to seek horses with desired qualities from distant parts of the world and maintain them in good condition even in an unsuitable environment, given the right food – and shelter. Management systems were beginning to evolve, and from the very beginning they were in response to man's alien demands rather than any requests put forward by the horse himself.

A scan across world breeds today show most countries in the Northern Hemisphere retain examples of their own supremely-adjusted indigenous breeds, some very ancient in origin. Other national breeds are more recent creations, conceived with jobs of work in mind. Most of the agriculture-based societies of northern Europe developed their own cold-blooded breeds of heavy draught horses for farm and haulage use, and lighter draught types for carriage horses with style and stamina.

The term cold-blood, used to describe the

'The Arab is considered by many to be the oldest and certainly one of the purest breeds in the world'

giant draught breeds, is a technical one that has nothing to do with body temperature and everything to do with temperament. It is derived from a German word *Kaltblutigkeit*, meaning 'calm and solid', and distinguishes the slow-moving, slow-thinking heavies from their spirited and fast-reacting hot-blood relatives who evolved in more open desert environments. In fact, the Arab and the Thoroughbred are the only true hot-bloods – the Arab being the progenitor of the Thoroughbred and considered by many to be the oldest and certainly one of the purest breeds in the world.

CHANGING ROLES

By the twentieth century redundancy notice had been served on the cold-blood workhorse in almost every one of his historical roles, and the future for the ancestors of the ancient 'forest horse' certainly looked bleak in comparison with the obvious attractions of the hot-blood for the new demands of sport and leisure riding. Numbers plunged, but as modern man's competitive urge threw up ever more variations on how to test the horse and rider partnership in every conceivable way, a positive avalanche of new 'warmblood' breeds have been created utilising cold-bloods to add strength, power, and a dose of common sense to the class and athleticism of the hot-bloods.

The vast majority of 'new' breeds can be grouped as warmbloods. Effectively, they are 'mongrels', developed by repeated crossing between hot-bloods, cold-bloods and other warmbloods to custom-create a specialist horse that will meet as closely as possible a particular sporting requirement. Though these breeds are artificial, thankfully for the horse, the priority has always been to produce an athlete that can move, breathe

and eat efficiently. This has saved the horse from the worst excesses of fashion that have affected dog showing.

The horse world has good reason to be proud of one truly synthetic creation – its elegant aristocrat, the Thoroughbred. Nature would certainly never have produced a horse so disastrously equipped for the rigours of the climate of England, where the breed was developed using a sprinkling of native genes blended into a cocktail of oriental, mainly Arab bloodlines. Yet, within barely 200 years, one of history's most strictly-controlled selective breeding programmes, together with the most intensive pampering, has created an all-round equine performer without equal. It has been used to 'upgrade' and refine almost every other horse breed and type, including many old strains, moulding them to more modern demands.

A recent survey illustrates the dramatic change in the role of the horse since the turn of the 20th century when the world's equine population still consisted almost exclusively of workers of one kind or another. From a total of 207 breeds today, only 36 are work horses, 67 are ponies and 104 are sports horses.

THE HORSE TODAY

Taller, faster, stronger, more graceful, more athletic, better tempered... today's horses are the result of centuries of domestication and genetic interference imposed upon millions and millions of years of evolution. So what, exactly, has that combination left us with? The answer is, an animal that is like, yet unlike, his wild ancestors. Like, in that beneath the cosmetic physical differences of shape, size and colour we still have a creature programmed for survival. He reacts, thinks and behaves as though every movement seen from the corner of his eye could be a predator about to spring and his next breath might be his last. The best chance of staying alive is to run – fast – or if trapped, let fire with everything he's got. He is super-alert himself, but he knows that he feels happiest and safest with other horses around him. His body systems tell him he should be grazing for the majority of the day, wandering about freely as he eats. The success of feral horses like the American mustangs, Australian brumbies or the ponies of the Camargue in southern France or in Chincoteague, show that, left well alone, even horses that have been genetically tampered with can do pretty well without our help by polishing these tried and tested tactics up to perfection once more.

However, these living skills would require some elbow grease to get working to full capacity again in the average domesticated horse. An early equus might admire the physique, beauty and jumping prowess of his modern-day counterpart, but he would be perfectly justified in looking down his nose at him when it came to mental agility. Over countless generations man has bred the kind of horses he wants, and all too aware of the horse's superior strength, he selected for breeding those animals inclined to be amenable and generally co-operative. Coupled with the humanising effect of growing up among people and being totally dependent for every need, we have created a species who – as far as the survival stakes go – has no worries. Most domestic horses, even 'unbroken' ones, are far less inclined to rush off or kick or bite ferociously under

pressure than feral horses or their truly wild ancestors. It is not only defensive reactions that have been blunted by selective breeding and training, natural 'street-savvy' seems to have been watered down too. Though it hardly seems possible in such a short evolutionary span, Susan McBane, author of many books on the horse, quotes studies that show ancient Przewalski horses had larger brains than those of recently-dead domesticated horses, and even of captive modern Przewalskis.

This is only one of many sacrifices the horse has made since taking up his lot with mankind. He has swopped his open horizon for four closed-in brick or wooden walls, his practically non-stop gentle exercise in the company of family and friends for the single life with an hour or two's excursion once a day, often going round and round in circles following his own tail, and his continual intake of nature's ideal food for two or three square meals of alien energy-producing substances with

> *'Perhaps the horse has just found the ultimate long-term survival technique'*

hardly a stalk of herbage in sight for hours in between. As if this was not enough, we have other bizarre expectations, such as presuming a horse should have no objection to having metal shoes nailed on his feet, to entering a box on wheels, to having a man sit on his back ordering him where to go and at what speed, asking that he keep jumping objects of considerable height that have perfectly good routes around the side of them, and demanding that he continually do as he is told, even when his every natural instinct tells him otherwise. It is only when we take all this on board that we begin to get some kind of perspective on how remarkably adaptable, amenable and generous the horse really is. Many might say that the horse must be essentially stupid to submit to such 'exploitation'. Looking at it from the horse's point of view, perhaps he has just found the ultimate long-term survival technique. After all, not many species have doubled their expected wild lifespan, guaranteed themselves protection against all natural predators, got food and water laid on and every ailment given care and attention, while still retaining a degree of independent aloofness.

Overall, so long as our expectations of his adaptability are reasonable, the deal 'ought' to come out in favour of the horse. Unfortunately, we often stretch our expectations to the very limits and beyond, and are then surprised that physical and psychological problems occur.

A SPECIAL RELATIONSHIP

Adaptability has been the horse's passport to survival in man's world. Like any bodily characteristics, flexibility and compliance have both been bred for and become increasingly engrained in equine make-up as time has gone by. Equally crucial to the horse's staying power, but maybe harder to pin down, is his extraordinary generosity and wish to please. After all, there is no reason why any horse should go along with any one of our weird and wonderful propositions. As every horseman or woman knows, even the smallest pony foal could turn down any request he considered unreasonable in no uncertain terms, if so inclined. When it comes to a battle of wills on physical terms there is no contest.

Part, but not all of the explanation, lies in the way that horse society itself is organised, where co-operation, not confrontation, is the key-word for herd living. So perhaps it is not so unusual for that affiliation be switched over to a horse-human bond when domestication threw the two of us together. However, there are many equally sociable herd animals who live in close contact with man, and few people expect the same friendship or loyalty from a cow or sheep that the horse gives so willingly.

What is the horse thinking of? Perhaps it is this intriguing mystery that underpins the unique, inspired relationship that has been forged between such totally different species as humans and horses. It is mind-boggling to conceive that a creature so strong, so swift-footed and so proud should allow us to borrow his power and grace and ask for so little in return. We still cannot quite believe it – and it makes for an irresistible and intense collaboration, with more than a touch of magic.

The horse enabled man to feel like a god. Sitting astride its galloping muscle-bound back, he must have felt invincible. From the beginning of time, before horses were even domesticated, the spell was already being woven as Stone Age peoples painted horses on the walls of their caves to conjure up spirits to help with the hunt. Since that time horses have been used in religious rituals, as sacrifices and have even been deified. The men who mastered the art of taming, harnessing and riding the horse gained speed and power beyond their wildest dreams. It is no wonder that horses took on supernatural powers in people's imaginations and became immortalised in legend and folklore across the world. Acknowledging its contribution to their supremacy, ancient civilisations prized and respected horses above all other animals, far more than just a useful tool. On a horse, a man became majestic, superior, authoritative – so horses became the symbols of status and wealth, the mounts of monarchs and knights.

Not a great deal has changed in the affluent societies of the 20th century where increased leisure time has simply provided new ways for the horse to fulfil man's aspirations. Horses are valued as highly as ever, and our admiration for the horse's spectacular beauty and pace is as great as ever. This enduring, special relationship has ridden out a complete reversal in the role of one of its major players and gone on to flourish as never before, in a much more even-handed game than war and hard labour had to offer.

Modern equestrian competition, in its many forms, has thrown horse and rider into ever-closer contact, each as dependent on the other in complete trust and understanding as the warrior and his war-horse once were. Horsemen and women intent on success at the highest level have to search for perfection in every detail of that partnership, for total harmony between man and horse. Central to achieving that harmony, whether performing Grand Prix dressage or simply hacking down the lane, is our ability to become listeners as well as talkers, starting to appreciate that communication is a two-way process.

Perhaps that is our challenge for the next century. For although the majority of horses are now loved with genuine affection, cared for and ridden better than ever before, we still have a tendency to view the horse in terms of what he can do for us. To achieve real partnership, maybe it is time to start appreciating the horse for his own sake, acknowledging how brilliant he is simply at being himself, and give him back something more than just shelter and food – respect for the remarkable, and remarkably generous, creature he is.

2 THE HORSE'S WORLD

The reason that the horse survived the rollercoaster of evolution so well, for so long, is largely down to the superb adaptation of its sensory mechanisms which co-ordinate to act as a highly sophisticated early warning system. In terms of evolutionary time, centuries of domestication are a mere blink of an eye. Although our horses may be more or less reactive and highly-strung, depending on their breeding and experience, the fundamental way this vital network functions has not changed at all. It might be an extremely long time since any domesticated horse had to worry about the threat of leopards and lions creeping up on him unexpectedly. Nevertheless, horses retain the hyper-sensitive equipment and reactions needed to keep a plains-dwelling prey animal alive. It is essential to understand the horse's world and appreciate how many equine reactions that may seem 'stupid' or deliberately awkward to us, are, in fact, automatic, virtually reflex responses. These have been programmed into his brain and nervous system so thoroughly that years of patient 'brainwashing' through training often cannot completely blot them out. The world, as the horse sees it, is sometimes the same as our own, but not always – and that is where the root of many misunderstandings between our two species lies. Even where similarities exist, we need to remember that the horse interprets what he sees, hears and feels in terms of his own needs, not ours, and his reactions are geared accordingly.

WHAT A HORSE SEES

A large area of the horse's cerebrum is devoted to data concerning sight, giving an indication of how important this ability is. Vision is the sense in which there are perhaps the greatest differences between our own perspective and that of the horses we ride and handle. Most obvious is the size of the horse's eyes and the way they are positioned on the head. Many experienced horsemen will say that the "eye is the window of the soul of a horse", and the horse's huge eyes – among the largest in size of all mammals and double the size of our own – are certainly part of his attraction to us.

The size and the placing of the eyes are typical of a hunted animal whose main concern is attack from behind. Both contribute to the horse's huge peripheral field of vision, which is far larger than a human's. A horse can see around 340 of the 360 degrees around it, from virtually any position – standing, eating or running. This leaves only two narrow blind-spots: one immediately behind, and the other, an area just in front of and beneath the nose. The blind-spot immediately behind the horse can be taken care of by a very slight angling of the raised head or rolling of the eye. Though a trained, mature horse learns to relax about things going on around and behind him, a nervous, edgy or young horse is likely to interpret any movement or noise from the rear as danger and either shoot forwards, swing round for a better view or, if panicked, kick out, just in case. Being able to see behind means, of course, that the horse can see most of the rider on his back too, something we often forget. He can see, as well as feel, what our legs, hands, body and whip are all doing, especially to the inside on a circle. It is not surprising how alarming it can be for a young horse, not sufficiently prepared, when a person sits on his back for the first time.

The second area blocked from view is two metres in front of and under the nose. This is why the sudden raising of a hand to pat the forehead is asking for a startled reaction. An approach at a slight angle to the shoulder gives the horse the best, and most reassuring, view. Coming from the front you tend to disappear at the crucial moment – so the horse, quite reasonably, turns away or steps sideways, not necessarily to avoid you but simply to get you back into his sight. This blind zone has obvious implications for the jumping horse, who can see the obstacle coming up clearly on the approach but then loses it from sight at the last moment, and, effectively, jumps a memorised image of its height and width. If the head is high up in the air the blind area increases, and, in any approach, a last-moment distraction in the sideways area of vision can be disastrous. By watching jumping horses you can see that many turn

The grazing horse's almost 360 degree field of vision means he can get on with the crucial business of eating, despite the threat of predators.

the head in the last stride to get a final look. Those who habitually approach dancing sideways are rarely accurate jumpers, because they cannot properly assess that all-important distance.

Although the peripheral field of vision is large, it is designed to pick up details of movement, rather than details of depth and dimension. The tiniest fluttering of a piece of paper in a hedgerow, caught in the corner of the eye, is sufficient excuse to put the body into instant alert with a shy – 'act first, think later' is the golden rule of the prey animal. Riders also notice how their horses will virtually fall over something right under their feet, yet can pick out the minutest of movements on the distant horizon and often tense up like a coiled spring, ready to react to possible danger. The side positioning of the eyes means that only a narrow zone in front of the horse is covered by both the eyes, thus providing a three-dimensional image. Spotting movement from a distance, giving those life-saving extra strides' headstart on a predator, is far more important in a life-death situation than good depth perception in the immediate vicinity, which is required by an effective hunter whose eyes are both placed on the front of the head, like ours.

Each equine eye works like a separate camera with a wide-angle lens, the right one capturing an almost completely different scene to the left. As a horizontal slit, the pupil is able to shrink in glaring light without ever reducing the scope of those far horizons. The corpora nigra, the dark blobs that can be seen floating in the eye, act like sunglasses helping to filter very bright sun.

So the horse's lateral vision is good, but monocular and therefore flat. His binocular vision, and ability to judge depth and distance, is limited to a very narrow range in front of him. The focusing mechanism itself is quite different to our own and often works against the horse in the work we now ask of him. In what seems a rather clumsy arrangement, the horse has to move his head in order to get things in clear

He may be tensing those neck muscles, but this gadget-bound youngster is working almost blind. His expression shows his lack of enjoyment of the whole process.

definition. The lens of a human eye is flexible, but the horse's lens has little adjustability. Therefore, to focus on objects at different distances, the horse has to position the light coming in through the pupil at the best possible point on the lens. Recent research has shown that the optimum place for the sharpest focusing is the middle of the retina, and the horse looks mainly through the upper section of his eye to facilitate this. As a result, he focuses best on objects in the middle distance. To get distant or very near objects into sharper view, he must either raise or lower his head, as he does when he scans across the skyline, or tucks in his nose and arches his neck to investigate a tidbit being offered.

It does not take much imagination to appreciate how this affects the ridden horse who is asked to hold his head perfectly still, often fixed rigidly in place by a variety of straps and gadgets. In the familiar surroundings and level surface of a manege, a mature horse may be comfortable with this, but a youngster is always likely to react with panic against such restriction, and understandably so. Any horse that is expected to gallop and jump over uncertain terrain must have the freedom of his head and neck, or, in effect, he is being partially blinded. Of course, the faster the horse is going, the less effective his focusing will be, and the same goes for the rider. The trained horse starts to adapt to constraint of his head movement by completing the picture using other sensory data, plus knowledge born of previous experience and trust in its trainer – but it all takes practice!

Another slight handicap, commonly affecting horses, is mild astigmatism. This occurs when the surface of the cornea does not curve in the normal way, so magnifying power in one direction is greater than in another. This produces a discrepancy between the vertical information and the horizontal information being received by the eye, and it means that although an object is seen vaguely, it cannot be fully 'assessed' right away. Again, the sensibly suspicious wild horse will make himself scarce before slowing down to weigh up a potential risk more fully. Translated to a riding situation, it is more considerate to allow a wary horse, especially a young one, time to stop and determine whether an alarming object is harmless or not, rather than immediately kicking on or raising the whip at the merest hesitation.

Several other features of the horse's vision are intriguing. It was once thought that horses were colour blind, but this is not the case. It has now been discovered that they are best equipped to see yellows and greens, are less handy at reds and blues, and not particularly good at violets and purples. Despite many riders' belief that their horse always seems to object to red fences or blue fences or whatever, what is more likely is that the horse is reacting either to something else about the fence, such as its unusual shape, or to the intensity of colour. They do seem more sensitive to extreme dark and extreme light, especially to the reflective glare of very white objects, which might mean they will spook at a white gate or paper bag, but will ignore a brown or even

'Good night vision is an obvious must for a prey animal, and the horse is no exception'

red objects. Good night vision is an obvious must for a prey animal, and the horse is no exception. The large eye gathers in maximum data and a special light-intensifying device, the tapetum lucidum, reflects light back on to the retina to make the most of what is available. We humans might expect a diurnal lifestyle of the horse, but in a natural state, he would be active through the night and use all his acute senses to gather the evidence needed about his surroundings in the dark. Though he might see quite well in dim light, it is thought that horses are considerably slower than we are at adjusting to a sudden change from dark to light or vice versa – a point worth remembering when you switch on the stable light at night, or expect your horse to leap without a second thought over a fence into a dark wood or walk straight into a gloomy box or trailer.

HOW A HORSE HEARS

The horse's ears are like radars, constantly swivelling in the direction of interesting sounds. In conjunction with sight, they are the mainstays of the defence system, as well as playing an important role in communication. Set high on the head, with superb mobility around 180 degrees, the external ears are built to pick up the slightest noise and precisely locate where it is coming from. They are far superior to our own fixed, rather second-rate appendages! Sixteen muscles control each ear, and by comparing the vibrations being funnelled in to each, the source of even very distant signals can be pinpointed with remarkable accuracy. Head and neck turned and ears pricked sharply in concentration, the horse is at maximum capacity for collecting in sound. Flattened during relaxation, sleep or, conversely, during extreme effort, the ears

can cut out unwanted background noise. Each can act totally independently of the other, one focusing on information coming from the front or the side, and the other concentrating on activity going on behind – such as what the rider is up to.

Internally, human and equine hearing mechanisms are much the same physically, but the horse can detect a far greater range of sound at both the higher and lower ends of the frequency scale, which extends to 25,000 cycles per second in comparison to our own 20,000 capacity. We have all known

Who goes there? Ears and eyes focus in combination on a source of interest – and possible danger.

The ears are highly mobile radars that can work together in intense concentration on a single point, or independently to cover two areas of interest. Here, one is forward on the photographer and direction of travel. The other listens to the rider's inside leg giving an aid to move sideways.

times when a horse detects that a friend is coming down the road long before we can hear the hoof beats – acutely sensitive hearing and precise sound location combining to superb effect.

Just as a horse whose ability to see is restricted is likely to become anxious and tense, one who cannot receive auditory signals easily also feels vulnerable. Still, calm days bring about an atmosphere of security and normality in the field, as sound carries well. Blustery days have the opposite effect, masking potential danger signals and so putting a group of horses on edge. As with sight, hearing is attuned to a horse's needs, drives and fears. Sounds that will interest him intensely may have no significance at all for us, and vice versa. So, background babble of human conversation is completely

ignored, while the slightest ominous rustle or shake of food in a bucket is guaranteed to put systems on red alert for flight or into a state of excited anticipation. Any unfamiliar sound is likely to be both worrying and fascinating to the horse. Sudden noises, particularly if they are loud, are certainly threatening and will create instant tension as the horse readies himself for escape. Often, especially with an older more worldly-wise animal, the horse decides perhaps there is no danger after all – then it's time for further investigation, with intense ear-pricked curiosity. Odd noises underfoot are always treated with suspicion, such as the hollow sound of his feet on a bridge or the trailer ramp, as the horse is always understandably nervous about where he places his precious feet.

As a rule, the sort of sounds a horse feels relaxed and safe about are low-level, regular noises. What is stressful is sheer volume, particularly if it is incessant, from heavy traffic or machinery for example, or constant bangings, clattering or shouting – all of which are jarring the nerves with painful stimuli and putting the whole body on constant stand-by.

Too often we fail to appreciate just how delicate the horse's hearing is. How many yards have raucous music blaring from the radio, dawn till dusk, with no consideration of how it is grating on the sensitive ears of the occupants, no doubt cringing in their stables, longing to be able to let themselves out and switch it off – or down, at least! That is not to say that horses have no musical appreciation; we know they have a strong sense of rhythm, but they do feel happiest and most at ease with calming, harmonious sound, rather than confusing, over-stimulating or abrasive noise.

By appreciating the horse's sense of hearing, we can make more effective use of it. For example, we take more advantage of his sensitivity to the human voice, as there are so many opportunities to do so. The voice can be an instrument of encouragement or chastisement, register a request, give a tactful warning of our approach, provide reassurance in a frightening situation, or simply strengthen the bonds of trust and confidence between us via a little conversation during grooming and handling. Most owners will confirm their horse seems to recognise their voice when they arrive at the yard in the morning, or even the noise of

their particular car engine – not surprising for an animal that can easily identify equine friends from individual neighs and whinnies.

Whenever the voice is used, it is tone and inflection that the horse is most sensitive to. "Whoa there...steady... w-a-a-l-king..." are soothing influences, where anything with an abrupt tone, such as "Terr-ott!", even if spoken softly, has an urgent, alerting, stirring up effect. We need to be conscious of this whenever we are talking around horses, whether speaking directly to them or not, and avoid being surprised or dishing out blame when they react to inflections in our voices likely to hype them up.

SENSE OF SMELL

Horses are very particular about who their friends are, and an initial meeting between two strangers is always touch and go. The ritual of establishing social contact is based on smell. The pair will approach each other with interest, but caution, extending noses from a safe distance to sniff the newcomer with great care. A sniff and a snort on both sides and breath is exchanged, sending a personal ID message from each horse deep into the other's nostrils, where it is duly analysed and memorised and a decision considered as to 'friend or foe'.

Housed in that elongated face, the nasal cavities are extensive, giving the horse a sensitivity to smells and their interpretation that we can hardly imagine. The large nostrils dilate to capture as much scent as possible, drawing it into the nasal chamber as the horse breathes in (which it does only

'Mares use scent-impression as their main method of distinguishing their own offspring'

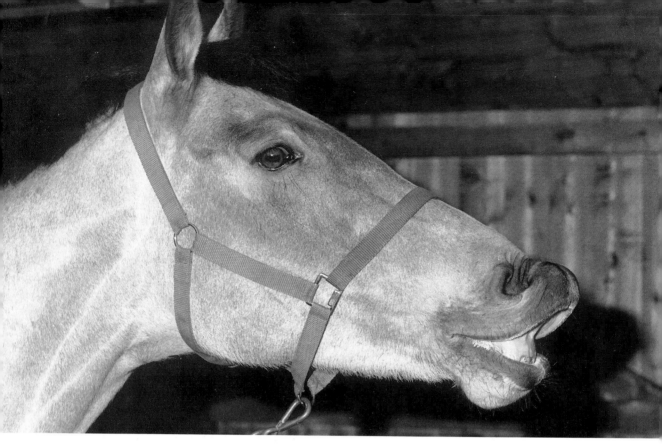

ABOVE: *The flehmen action pushes particularly interesting scents back into the ultra-sensitive Jacobsen's organ.*

BELOW: *Rolling helps 'grind' the herd smell into the coat and skin.*

through its nose, not the mouth). There, the air is exposed to the olfactory nerve cells as it is passed across coils of bone covered with mucous membranes lined with tiny hairs. Airborne information, processed by the sense of smell, is significant to horses in many important ways, not only for communication and recognition. A wild horse must know the odour of a lurking or approaching predator, be able to home in on the presence of water that could be far from sight, and sense when he is within his own herd's territory as marked by their dunging. Familiarity equals security, so from a horse's point of view, he is happiest in a stable that has his own aroma about it, not that of another horse. The most natural thing to do to a bed of fresh straw is to mark it with one's own odour – much to the frustration of a stable-proud owner!

The horse's digestive system is ill-equipped to handle mistakes, so smell and taste work closely together in ensuring the most nutritious plants and grasses are eaten and harmful vegetation is avoided. Unfamiliar smells are considered ominous and their source best ignored, as any owner who has tried to give antibiotic powders in the feed is well aware. Food-type scents are understandably important to horses; they are keenly sensitive to them and have no trouble at all sniffing out a lone pony nut at the bottom of a coat pocket.

Crucial to males is the ability to identify mares in heat. A stallion is able to detect the enticing fragrance of an in-season mare at a distance of up to 200 metres. Once he gets within sniffing distance and prepares to begin courtship, more accurate evidence is needed as to his chosen one's receptiveness. This is when the Jacobsen's organ comes into play. This is a special hollowing of the nasal cavity super-sensitive to pheromones, the scent messages that carry information on another animal's sexual condition, its emotional state and personal identity. A deep inhalation is needed to drive air into these vomeronasal organs, so whenever such a smell requires close investigation, the horse performs the 'flehmen' action. By curling his top lip and closing the nostrils, he forces the scent-heavy air around these pits to savour and thoroughly analyse the data it contains. Stallions use flehmen extensively in pre-mating manoeuvres, but it can be seen displayed in many circumstances where horses are intrigued by a strong, strange or unfamiliar odour, or even in an odd situation which is puzzling them where they are trying to pick up as many clues as possible about what is going on. Pheromones are produced by glands in the skin and are also present in the coat oils, urine, faeces, breath and sweat. Among the many specific meanings they can convey is fear; a scent that horses certainly seem able to detect in both other animals and humans and which is, not surprisingly, extremely infectious, immediately alerting the fight or flight response.

'The world of a horse, like a dog's, is full of scent messages that he will actively seek out'

Mares use scent-impression as their main method of distinguishing their own offspring, particularly at night when there are no visual indicators and the herd is quiet. At birth the foal is methodically licked and sniffed all over to establish its personal fragrance, and daily nuzzles reinforce the bond, enabling the mare to adjust its image as the foal grows. Smell language generally plays a major part in keeping the herd together by providing a subtle means of communication and recognition, and horses use it constantly in many ways every day of their lives. One of the reasons for rolling, for example, is thought to be an individual's urge to cover itself with the group smell and increase its sense of 'belonging'. This is a dimension of the horse's life to which we give scant attention, probably because, having such poor olfactory ability ourselves, we attach little importance to it. The world of a horse, like a dog's, is full of scent messages that he will actively seek out to help build an image of his surroundings. We, in comparison, only use information about scent when it quite literally hits us on the nose!

To a horse, a quick sniff-over is his natural 'getting to know you' technique. Yet, how many of us approach a strange horse quietly, stand still and allow him to make his mind up that way rather than striding up to slap him heartily on the neck, without so much as a by your leave ? How much more at ease horses new to each other would be if we provided a safe opportunity for them to get acquainted with a whiff rather than insisting on them keeping their noses apart and them minding their own business for the sake of 'good manners'?

HOW HORSES USE TASTE

Taste is connected closely to the sense of smell; it is used mainly in feeding in the same way as it is for us. Groups of cells called the taste buds are collected at the end of each taste nerve fibre, situated mainly on the tongue but also around the palate and throat. Information is passed to the brain as degrees of four flavours – salt, bitter, sweet and sour – and by adding these impressions to those of smell and texture, a complete impression of a substance is built up. Sweetness and saltiness seem to be the favoured tastes, with sourness and bitterness disliked, perhaps because most poisonous or unpalatable plants have a bitter flavour. Nevertheless, some horses can be amazingly tolerant of bitterness and have even been known to develop a passion for fence preservatives or the preparations painted on their stable woodwork to discourage chewing!

'Smell and taste work together, especially in bonding between individuals'

As mentioned previously, horses eat fussily and are wary of unfamiliar smells or tastes, which, as they are incapable of being sick, is very sound policy. Their incredibly sensitive and mobile lips help sort out and discard substances deemed unsuitable, whether it is a patch of particularly unsavoury grass or worming granules mixed as thoroughly as possible into the feed bucket. Dry, sour feed, caked around the edges of bowls, stale, unfamiliar water, or the slightest taint of chemical or detergent on a bucket can put off a particularly sensitive feeder. Smell and taste work together as a means of communication, especially during bonding between individuals such as during the mutual grooming of friends, the licking of the foal by its mother, and the biting and chewing of a stallion and mare during courtship.

It is not known, with certainty, how far the two senses work independently of each other in these circumstances.

40

TOUCH, FEELING AND SENSATION

Touch adds a further dimension to the world with which the horse has direct contact, but it is not the only kind of 'feeling' ability that a horse has. All kinds of 'feelings' are received by groups of specialised cells, known as sense receptors, and these fall under several groupings.

Firstly, there are the feelings of pressure, pain and temperature which are external stimuli received by the exteroceptors. Sensory cells in the eyes, nose, mouth and ears are also specialised receptors of this type, receiving signals from outside the horse. However, the touch, pain and heat/cold sense cells are mainly situated within the skin, spread across the body in groups of varying densities and proportions of each type of cell.

The nose and muzzle, for example, are extremely sensitive to touch pressure via the whiskers, with sensory cells and nerve endings highly concentrated here. Picking up sensation is one function of all types of body hair, but the whiskers are the ultimate antennae, crucial for taking in data about the immediate area around and underneath the nose, which the horse's elongated face blocks from view. Whiskers help judge the distance from the nose to the ground, and they evaluate the textures of plants and other foodstuffs before they are taken into the mouth. From the horse's perspective, these valid uses for whiskers far outweigh the human being's excuses for chopping them off in the name of 'tidiness'. Other areas, such as the neck, withers, shoulder and back of the lower legs, are also known to be particularly touch-sensitive, far more so than the sides of the rib-cage where the rider's legs rest. Pain sensors are concentrated around the mouth, and so the gums are easily desensitised by rough hands or bad bitting. The feet's speciality appears to be a hyper-alertness to surface vibrations – after all, the horse's continued existence relies upon staying upright whatever the ground beneath his hooves.

All sensory cells are connected by an intricate network of nerves to the central nervous system – that is, the spinal column and ultimately the brain, its headquarters. The cells work by registering a stimulus. Once the stimulus reaches a certain level of intensity, the cells are triggered to relay a message to the brain via an impulse along the nerves. Like a computer, the brain receives the information, stores it, interprets it and makes a decision on action. This instruction is then sent in further (motor) impulses back down the nerves to the muscles, ordering them how to respond. Routine and experience combine to build up a memory-bank of stimuli and responses which then help dictate reactions.

Sensitivity to all kinds of stimuli varies between individual horses and between different parts of the body. Some horses, those with hot-blooded ancestry in particular, have thin skins which leave the sensory receptor cells close to the surface and so more exposed. Certain body areas are thinner-skinned than others in all horses, or better supplied with nerve endings and therefore especially sensitive and ticklish.

'Tactile stimulation is clearly important to horses, as they use it extensively in communication'

Insisting on scrubbing away at the vulnerable under-belly, for example, with a stiff-bristled brush is asking for a reaction, so it is totally unfair to reprimand the horse for swishing its tail or kicking out in annoyance at such an unprovoked assault!

Tactile stimulation is clearly important to horses, as they use it extensively in communication between themselves, and they clearly enjoy and respond to it when we relate to them in this way, not only through considerate grooming but the general 'getting to know you' rubs and scratches that horses themselves use. Sensitive noses touch often within the herd situation – between mares and foals, friends or strangers meeting. Bonds are strengthened with 'mutual grooming', the rubbing, nibbling ritual that can be observed within any settled and relaxed group, and touch sensation plays a major role in courtship and mating. Being able to touch, as well as to see other horses can make all the difference between happiness and extreme anxiety for a stabled horse.

'Bonds are strengthened with mutual grooming...the rubbing, nibbling ritual'

Besides the sensory cells that react to external, physical pressures or stimuli, there are two further kinds of feeling sensations at work at all times in the horse's body. Interoceptor cells are not concerned with touch, but respond to internal changes. Included in this category are receptors sensitive to pain and discomfort, but also cells lining the digestive system programmed to react to concentrations of chemicals. Organic sensations bring bodily need to the animal's attention – hunger, thirst, tiredness, the urge to breed, defecate or urinate, for example.

A further sensation, which all animals share, is body awareness. None of us would survive very long, least of all a flight animal, if we were constantly having to concentrate on what position our limbs were in relation to each other, to the rest of our body and to the ground. Proprioceptor cells respond to stimuli within the joints, muscles, tendons and ligaments, enabling the horse to assess his position and relationship to the ground as these stretch and tense. In this way, he can control and co-ordinate movement without giving it a conscious thought. Working in conjunction with the organs of balance in the ear, the horse stays on his feet throughout changes of body position, direction and pace, by producing involuntary reflexes which activate muscles to maintain the body's equilibrium. Muscles in the head and neck are especially important in balance.

All creatures have this rather amazing subconscious ability, but it is something at which the horse, a creature that evolved on the basis of motion and finely-tuned co-ordination, is an expert. Although a newborn foal is slightly clumsy and awkward, in comparison to most infant mammals, his paces are relatively well-developed according to an in-built, inherited pattern that will enable him to be up and following the herd within minutes of birth. As time goes by and the body grows, the brain computes the changing relationships of the limbs, body and ground, and continues to adjust to them, according to the horse's experience with other horses and with humans, and his movements become more and more established and regulated.

Further alterations are needed, of course, each time a rider gets on to his back, which again has to come with experience and good training to help him adjust as easily as possible.

THE TELLINGTON THEORY

Linda Tellington-Jones travels the world demonstrating her unique Tellington-Touch Equine Awareness Method, and working with horses at all levels from 'ordinary' hacks to the German Olympic dressage team. Her techniques involve a whole new approach to the way that a horse thinks, reacts and learns, based on the workings of the nervous system. The TT.E.A.M system of gentle, non-invasive manipulations and ground exercises, aimed at increasing body awareness, were inspired by her four years of study with the Israeli physicist Moshe Feldenkrais. Seeing how human bodies, paralysed by pain, could be helped by 're-organising' the nervous system to open up 'non-habitual' nerve pathways, Linda was convinced that the same principles could be applied to horses. Many resistances for which horses were often punished or even written off actually stemmed from pain or stress-induced bodily tension that prevented the horse thinking rationally about his situation. When the horse is in pain or conflict, he reacts instintively in one of four ways: flight, fight, freeze or faint. By using body awareness techniques to re-route impulses along newly-activated, alternative neural routes, this paralysing effect could be released and the panic reflex over-ridden. Instead of acting blindly and instinctively,

the horse could quite literally be 'taught to think' – and, in addition, increase his learning capacity.

Believing that it is time for us to take a completely new look at the horse, giving him credit for his intelligence and generosity. Linda says:

' I think that one of the reasons why people have not appreciated the use of touch with the horse is that they don't like being touched themselves. They are nervous about it and, unless you come from the southern countries, it is not accepted. We just do not think about reaching out and touching. We spend very little time, if any, watching horses together when they are loose, and seeing how much they touch. Yet, in many parts of the world, trainers say 'Don't touch the horse, you will spoil him'.

I find there is so little understanding of the horse's potential intelligence or willingness to co-operate. There are some real myths, such as 'horses are out to get you' and you have to dominate them. This is a very common mode of thinking in the majority of training situations. What I have discovered is that when you use information new to the nervous system, in a way that takes a horse beyond its instinctive Flight-Fight-Freeze-Faint, then the horse actually really enjoys co-operating.

We all accuse animals of having intentional resistance. It is not intentional, it is neurological. People should realise that there is another possibility other than dominating the horse. I never think of a horse as being intentionally aggressive, but

'We are still in the dark ages with horses...not taking into consideration how the brain works'

ABOVE: *Linda Tellington-Jones uses a light, white dressage whip, which she calls a 'wand', to calm the horse and focus its attention This is part of her system of ground exercises for improving body awareness.*

RIGHT: *Linda believes that pain or tension in the horse's body can cause the resistances commonly labelled intentional or unchangeable. Her system of non-invasive manipulations helps the horse to break out of this vicious circle. Here, she explores the horse's body for signs of stress.*

Photos: John Birt.

it is more likely to be holding tension or fear somewhere in the body and is trying to protect itself. Hitting or yelling will only deepen the tension.

Many people who get into horses do it because they love animals, and yet when they enter the horse world, what are they told? In the majority of cases, it is that you constantly have to get after the horse and he has to be controlled. Now, I think that is true if you don't find a common ground and a place of respect and understanding. It is like ballroom dancing – if someone isn't leading, it doesn't work. Certainly, in the beginning, you have to be very clear about what it is you want. But there are many instances once you get beyond that point that the horse can become so tuned in to you and so intelligent that he is then able to take turns. Fear stays in the cellular memory for years. How a horse is worked through a problem when he is young lays the whole foundation of whether he is going to look to you to help to overcome a fear, or whether he learns he will only get beaten for it.

We are still in the dark ages with horses – not taking into consideration how the brain works, how the nervous system works. It is just a question of 'if a horse resists hit him', not 'how can we help him to learn to co-operate and learn how to learn'. If you touch the horse all over in a kind way, so they overcome their fear, you give them new information about themselves. The touch brings a new self-awareness and self-confidence, so that the animal is able to think more effectively, no matter what you ask him to do, because you can over-ride his fear reflex and take him beyond instinct. You can release fear or memory of pain at a cellular level.

When you awaken differentiated areas of the body with these circular touches all over, rather than the long strokes of a massage, what happens is an activation of more than the average neural impulses. Think of the brain as being connected to all those parts of the body to which we are bringing feeling. It is like turning on the electric light of the terminal in the brain. The animal dares to turn around and look and see itself – they have a different physical self-image and so, self-confidence.

When a horse goes into flight, the nervous system is activated and the blood rushes up to the big muscles in the shoulders and tops of the legs, so the horse is ready for action.

This limits the horse's self-image because they cannot feel their connection to the ground. Then, if they tighten their hindquarters, their back or neck, the impulses that go through the body are also being blocked, so the horse cannot feel his body so well. He is cut off from his own physical feelings. It is this awareness that we are trying to reactivate with the touches and the other exercises.

When all a horse has is flight or fight, the choices are not there. If the horse is given choices and shown how to use them, he will use them. When you give a being new tools to function with other than instinct, my experience is that the animal will use the new information instead of reacting back to flight. He might still flee, but it will be a conscious choice rather than a freak-out. Because intelligence takes over, the effect is permanent.

When I first started talking about increasing animals' intelligence twenty years ago, I was really criticised and told that only human beings can have intelligence. The fact is, that intelligence is the ability to adapt to new situations. Horses are very good at that and they can become much better if you can let them know what it is you want, and only ask them to do what is reasonable.

People in the horse world don't tend to think that horses can think. Through the research that has been done in England by Maxwell Craig using the 'mind mirror' we now know that using these circular touches helps the creature go beyond instinct, activating the brainwaves we humans use

'If the horse is given choices and shown how to use them, he will use them'

for logical thinking. With alpha brainwaves alone a person cannot learn, even if they are concentrating, because the learning is not retained unless the beta waves are present. I could hardly believe it! Why did it take us so long to find out that horses actually have the capability of thinking in just the same brainwave patterns as we do? It is this attitude that we humans are 'superior' and that we are not really animals.

What has now been discovered is that the limbic system, the part of the brain that controls the emotions, is also the seat of learning. I think what happens with this work is that you get a regulation of the emotions, a smoothing out back to the ability to make choices. As a consequence, learning is accelerated. An animal that is highly emotional and highly charged does not learn well – you find yourself having to repeat things over and over again.

At first it didn't cross my mind that you could affect the personality or behaviour of the horse by working on the body. It was not until I started training in the summer of 1975, working on the human nervous system using the Feldenkrais method, that I suddenly got it. It was absolutely possible to change the learning capacity of the horse, its willingness to cooperate and its athletic ability. So it is fascinating, a totally new way of thinking about horses – and it works. Anyone can do the touches and with great results.

However, where there is discomfort or pain – either man-made or due to a fault in conformation – it is not enough to only work on the body alone. You have to teach the horse to move in a new way so habitual ways of responding are overcome. We must help the horse to do things differently so it makes it better for him. What I like best about the work is that it has helped some of the best riders in the world, but even the average person who is having a little difficulty with their horse can mess around with the touches and discover how much more co-operative the horse can be. We can all come to a new understanding with the horse. **,**

SIXTH SENSE

Do horses have a sixth sense? Many people believe they do, even going so far as to say that they are telepathic or able to use psychic, or extra-sensory perception. Much well-observed horse behaviour is certainly not easy to explain using existing scientific rationale. However, we have so much to learn about the way horses use their senses, as their equipment is so different to our own, that it is difficult to say that what appears a super-sensory phenomenon cannot be put down to heightened acuity of the conventional senses. Homing instinct, for example, is a fascinating topic that has been reported in numerous instances. It was thoroughly investigated in a series of controlled experiments by Moyra Williams, an expert on equine psychology, who concluded that in cases where visual memory could not operate, smell was the sense most likely to be used in homing, with the horse relying on minute windborne clues to suggest the direction it should take.

Horses certainly seem to detect changes in

'The way that we stand, move and approach speaks volumes to the horse'

the weather approaching, an ability useful in the wild, and they have been known to sense and avoid radio-activity. Their famous ability to pick up on human moods and states of mind, is probably largely down to a keen awareness of detail, whether it be visual, auditory, olfactory, or a combination of several or all the senses. Tension and anxiety, as all horse people know, passes like an electric current down the reins or even across space, as clear a signal as it is possible to give to a flight animal whose second name is 'nervousness'. At the opposite extreme, some people undeniably have a feel for, or 'way' with horses, largely due to the reassuring effect of the calm confident air they have about them. The way that we stand, move and approach speaks volumes to the horse, whose language is built up nuances of body position and muscular tension.

A horse may not have a creative imagination, but he does possess excellent powers of association, so it is easy to comprehend how the appearance and scent of a vet is good reason to avoid being caught, or putting on the travelling boots could mean an exciting day's competition, so breakfast suddenly loses its appeal. As we have found, human senses are so poorly developed in comparison with those of such a successful escape artist, that we are not in a very strong position to judge what a horse can detect and what he cannot.

3 PATTERNS FOR LIVING

What makes a horse act like a horse? What are the urges, needs and preoccupations that provoke and drive the way he behaves? If we are choosing to share and shape his world as completely and radically as we attempt to, then we ought to make every effort to discover the answers to these questions.

As evolution was gradually moulding the physiology of the horse, the mind and behaviour were evolving in tandem to create between them the essential flight animal. Selective breeding over 250 centuries may have cosmetically altered the body of equus, but it has barely scratched the surface of 55 million years worth of genetic programming of his basic behavioural codes. Those patterns for living and surviving have served him well. From the horse's point of view, why change a successful formula? So let us look at, and try to understand, what makes this animal tick. In doing so, we might have to alter more than a few of our ideas of what we think makes him happy and at ease with his world.

Broadly speaking, all horse behaviour is inspired by four overwhelming needs: to eat and drink, to stay alive, to reproduce and to socialise with his own kind.

FOOD AND WATER

Top of the priority list for every living being is the absolutely fundamental requirement of eating and drinking. Accordingly, the process takes on a central importance in behaviour, and the finding and consuming of food preoccupies most animals – ourselves and horses included. The need to drink is even more pressing than the need to eat. More than any other aspect of management, feeding and watering can affect a horse's physical and psychological health and happiness, yet the difference between his natural diet and the feeding regime imposed on modern domesticated horses could hardly be greater.

Most significant of all is the fact that, given the opportunity, a free-roaming horse will graze for a minimum of twelve hours per day. Steadily sifting and picking across the available vegetation with his mobile lips, he will select a low-quality but varied intake of leaves, plants, herbs and grasses to fulfil his nutritional needs. In preference horses will feed for at least sixteen hours out of twenty-four, whether hungry or not, because the code in their genes tells them to do so. Research has proved that, whatever the quality of the pasture, the horse will continue the grazing action until his psychological need to chew has been satisfied. So the occupant of a lush paddock will keep eating for a full sixteen hours, just

Free-living horses will spend most of their day eating, moving about and socialising – that is, doing what comes naturally.

as he would if the enclosure was almost bare and he had to search for his food, and he would continue grazing long after his hunger or nutritional need is fulfilled. Hence the ease with which ponies, in particular, get overweight. The horse eats and chews slowly, not only because the selection process should not be rushed, but because the flight animal's stomach is small. Little by little food is nibbled, ground up and swallowed, and trickles almost continuously through the digestive system. Neither the stomach nor the gut bacteria, which process the food within the intestines, can tolerate either sudden dramatic change to the diet or long periods without anything to work on. When the system is empty or near empty, the horse cannot relax.

So, the horse is physically designed and mentally programmed for the consumption of varied, low-grade fibrous forage, and for spending at least two-thirds of his day processing it. The contrast with the daily regime of most stabled horses could not be starker. A diet of high-quality concentrate grain presented by the bucketful three times a day to conveniently fit in with our mealtimes, may be more than adequate in terms of nutritional value – but as far as behavioural needs go, the horse is practically being starved. Finishing his manger or bucket within minutes and his haynet inside a couple of hours, he is then left to stand between his four walls with little to occupy his thoughts, and even less to occupy his digestion, for the next third or more of his day. What is the sense in meeting those dietary needs so quickly with high-grade food when the horse's natural urges tell it to go on and on eating, whether it has already had the appropriate nutritional intake or not?

It is remarkable how many horses do come to suppress their natural instincts and tolerate the artificiality of their domesticated routine, though it is interesting to note that colic is virtually unknown in wild-living horses. Every yard, however, has its examples of frustrated individuals who cannot adapt or whose tolerance threshold is low – the weavers, crib-biters and wind-suckers, desperate to fill their hours with activity and their stomachs with absolutely anything, even if it is only air. More frequent, smaller, concentrate feeds and a greater proportion of forage, given in such a way that it takes much longer to obtain in small amounts, are simple measures that would go a long way to 're-naturalising' feeding programmes, while still catering for modern, controlled, high-energy demands. The type of food provided, and the time given to eat it, is at the root of the majority of behavioural problems, and there are as many difficulties that can be traced to over-feeding of an excessively energy-rich a diet as there are related to under-nourishment.

However urgent their need, horses will not eat or drink indiscriminately. When grazing they will instinctively choose to eat what the body needs and reject what is not required, or what might possibly cause harm. Feeding is a somewhat risky business for an animal that has no ability to vomit. Appetite varies

between individuals and can be as easily affected by the animal's mental state as his physical requirements. An agitated horse cannot settle to his feed, whether the reason is anticipation of excitement, or anxiety, perhaps caused by the threat from another more dominant horse or from lack of company. Many factors can distract a horse from his food. After all, if there is the slightest possibility that flight may be required, then it is better not to spend too much time eating – that can wait until the coast is clear.

It follows that the horse that is not settled and content in his environment is not going to eat well and thrive. So much time, effort and investment is put into the scientific analysis of the horse's nutritional requirements, the specifications of types of feedstuffs in nutrient content, digestible energy, etc., yet scant notice is given to this fundamental truth. If the horse is not happy – not only with his feeding regime but in his whole lifestyle – then this is going to have a detrimental effect on his appetite and therefore his physical condition. How many 'bad-doers' are simply worried horses whose owners have not given enough time and thought either to a more natural feeding routine, or to evaluating the personality of the animal and discovering what will help him feel settled enough to eat up well?

> '*A horse that is not settled and content is not going to eat well and thrive*'

Another interesting and misunderstood aspect of the motivation to eat is the use of food and tidbits in education. This all-important basic drive ought to be a most persuasive and useful training tool – after all, a dog can be taught to do almost anything if the prospect of a tidbit is in sight, and a child will do anything asked in return for a sweet. The response of the child or the dog, however, is the reaction of a carnivore to the thought of a meal – a reward he would literally kill for! The herbivore has a totally different perspective on food, one which dilutes the effectiveness of feed as a means of positive reinforcement. His dinner is all around him all the time, he nibbles it all day long, his stomach is (or should be) continually partly full of it – what difference does one extra mouthful make? That is not to say that tidbits are not appreciated; they give the horse short-term satisfaction, help to divert his attention from an uncomfortable task, or make him well-disposed towards the person whose pockets they appear from. As an enticement to perform a task well, however, a horse could not be less interested.

Monty Roberts, summing up forty years experience of training horses in the most non-invasive way possible, says: "Herbivores can't associate food with activity very well at all. You can teach a horse to go to get food, but there is almost no activity you can get him to do, and then look for a food reward as a result. You can't get him to work for food. You can give him a mint and he'll enjoy it – but all you have taught him to do is to pull your shirt off to find the mint!"

SELF-PRESERVATION

A horse that feels threatened cannot concentrate on eating, as he cannot concentrate on anything, because his whole continued existence hinges on his need to protect himself. In the open grassland environment of his evolution this means his ability to run, and run fast, from the merest hint of danger. There are no second chances for the prey animal – hesitation could be fatal. The knowledge that he represents a good dinner to some extremely cunning and lethal hunters caused the horse to develop his most powerful instinctive reaction – flight. There is a second defensive option at the horse's disposal, which is fight, in the form of feet, teeth and an almighty buck. But a clean escape is always preferable to exposing yourself to possible injury or defeat, so horses will choose flight above fight in almost every instance, unless cornered when the option of making themselves scarce is closed to them. Movement is their preferred solution to most problems. Those all-important feet are the getaway vehicle and so they are guarded closely from risk. No foot, no escape – so any horse that willingly lifts its feet to be cleaned, or even steps out without hesitation on to a strange, untested surface is showing a degree of trust and confidence that goes against a deeply ingrained rule of thumb.

The self-preservation instinct is so strong that it can be set off by the slightest threat, real or imagined. That is what represents a threat to the horse's mind, not to a human one. From the fluttering paper in the hedgerow to the whip on his quarters, the urge to flee dominates all other considerations until the horse considers itself out of danger.

Hand in hand with the drive for self-preservation is the need for freedom to flee. Enforced idleness must be a torture for any naturally free-roaming animal, but most stressful and frightening of all is closing off all his escape routes. The cosy stable that is our idea of comfort and security is effectively a cage to a horse, who is programmed to function in the wide open spaces, among other horses, and constantly on the move. Though most horses resign themselves to confinement, some show clear signs of stress that are often ignored or put down to an unsociable temperament. Bad temper does seem to be more common among stabled horses. How often is it due to apprehension and sheer frustration in a horse that has no means of avoiding the source of its annoyance? At least a field-kept horse can evade being caught.

By nature, the horse is extremely claustrophobic, because being shut in any small, enclosed space exposes him to risk. Direct restraint can also be a source of trauma. Most horses will learn to lead and tie happily with sympathetic handling, but tying on too short a rack or bearing down on a tight leadrope is asking for a panic reaction when the fear of restriction kicks in and the flight-fight response takes over. Often, just a little more length to allow the head and neck freedom of movement and the horse a chance to see properly is enough to provide reassurance.

STRESS AND STEREOTYPES

Any animal who is prevented by confinement from doing what comes naturally risks developing the obsessive, repetitive behaviours that are called stereotypes. These include weaving, cribbing, box-walking or even head tossing or banging the door. These are all ways of coping with the stress that their circumstances have created. Stereotypes are unknown in horses living in the wild or solely at pasture, yet they are common in stabled horses fed concentrate diets and given little or no chance to fill their days with meaningful equine activity.

GILLIAN O'DONNELL'S VIEW

Gillian O'Donnell (using the pen-name Susan McBane) is a prolific writer on equestrian topics with some 20 books to her credit, including A Natural Approach to Horse Management. *In 1978 she co-founded, with Moyra Williams, the Equine Behaviour Study Circle, a society for people interested in horse behaviour which has members worldwide and regularly contributes to behavioural research.*

Gillian is outspokenly critical of the general lack of appreciation of the essential nature of the horse and of his real needs when it comes to modern management systems.

' On the whole, people are not trying hard enough to think like a horse and understand what a horse is going through when it is managed in the conventional way. The worst reason for doing anything is because 'it's always been done that way'. Sometimes there are better ways, and it is up to every owner to look around and decide how to bring together the best of the new and best of the old. Owners must really try to observe and get to know their horses as animals and as individuals, and then think to themselves: if they were that animal, would they be happy?

The area probably in direst need of attention is accommodation and the length of time that many horses are left in stables. Horses are horses. They are not dogs – they don't have dens in the wild and they do not like being in a confined space. True, they appreciate shelter, and I am not saying it is

'I am not saying that it is cruel to stable horses, but most horses are in their stables too long'

Clean and tidy – but, oh, so boring. Traditional stable yard design has little to do with the horse's behavioural and psychological needs and everything to do with human convenience.

cruel to stable horses, but most horses are in their stables too long, and the stables are too small, uncomfortable and poorly ventilated. If people were more sensitive to these issues there would not be half the health and behavioural problems there are. Unfortunately, for many owners using livery yards there is little choice, but there are areas that are easy to improve, such as providing more exercise and more forage feed.

If you walked down any line of stables at any time other than feed time and opened all the doors, what would happen? All the horses would walk straight out! That is what horses need – they need freedom and they need company. Of course they can settle to living in a stable if they are exercised properly and fed properly, but this so rarely happens. They get used to it, but I'm sure

that is only resignation. And the more sensitive ones become ratty and defensive and start stable vices.

The horse sees the conventional loose-box as nothing short of a prison, but it is difficult to find stables designed with the horse's needs in mind. How often do you see stables where horses can touch each other? Why ever not? They touch each other all the time out in the field. They maintain eye contact for 80 per cent of the time outside, yet they cannot do that at all in almost all ordinary stables. Horses feel safer and more secure when they have an all-round view, and for that reason there should be more than one outlook from every horse's stable. How often do you find a modern stable where the horse can see 365 degrees around him? Research done on stabled horses found they were much more settled and ate more when they were all kept together loose in a large barn. The manufacturers of products like stabling talk a lot about their workmanship but seem to give no thought at all to design. They have never looked into a horse's mind and seen how the horse sees things.

Over-confinement, over-feeding and not ensuring the horse is more comfortable are, I believe, the worst and most common mistakes that are made. Rugs, for example, are a huge bugbear to me. Many rugs are like straitjackets to horses! If you were constantly having to wear clothes that were irritating to you, were confined in a tiny space when you needed to be walking around all the time, and were not feeding the way you would feed yourself by choice and so were feeling hungry most of the time, you would be totally miserable.

For some reason we simply don't feed horses like horses. Feed companies need to be concentrating on providing a much wider variety of nutritious and palatable forages. The alfalfa chop now available is good, but still overlooks the fact that many horses dislike alfalfa. We should not need to mix it with heavily molassed products like sugar beet to get our horses to eat it. I would like to be able to offer my horse food that she likes and wants to eat.

Concentrate feeds also tend to contain many additives and the grain has been grown using pesticides and chemical fertilisers. We need a lot more organically grown feeds, because I believe many health problems we now face, such as allergies, are down to the way feed is grown and prepared. And I would question why feed companies promote so many cereal-based feeds that are not right and natural for horses. Things are improving, for example with the haylage products now available, but there is a long way to go. Frustration and discontent

Management-related stress creates the unhappiness that shows itself in stereotyped behaviours such as stable vices. A wind-sucker is desperate to fill his stomach.

because the horse is not being treated in a way that is appropriate to its mentality and physique, are undoubtedly the root causes of the majority of health and behavioural problems faced by today's owners and riders.

Horses are so adaptable and so stoical when you consider the kind of life many of them lead. Most problems stem from management and I believe this is even more important than the way we ride, because the management applies to every minute of every day. You can't hope to get a decent relationship with your horse if the management is wrong, because you will never get it performing right.

I think that most horses, if they are ridden and managed sympathetically, like working. They like being with us and are interested in going for rides and being active, provided they are happy. On the whole, horses that are not working are bored to tears, because even in a field there isn't enough room for them to lead a truly natural life. Yes, they do need company of their own kind, but they are perfectly capable of building up a very good relationship with a human and to looking forward to going out and being ridden, if everything is sympathetically done. Unfortunately, too often, it is not, and so problems result.

Understanding and appreciating the horse's real nature and real needs is the crucial element in the partnership, but awareness seems to be sadly lacking amongst novices and professionals alike. There are so many unhappy owners and unhappy horses around, purely due to a lack of basic knowledge and thought about the kind of animals horses are. People need to study the animal before they start doing anything with it. For example, we ought to say to ourselves: 'As I intend to ride this animal, I need to understand what his back is like. And in view of what I now know, does this saddle I'm about to use actually fit?' Most saddles are actually too narrow due to the fashion for a narrow twist that developed in the sixties.

To be able to look at things like this from a horse's point of view people do need education, which is why I believe riding schools should first give everyone who comes to learn to ride a lesson on the ground on what the horse is, emphasising that horses only do as we ask because they are very well trained. I wouldn't dream of walking into a lion's cage and suddenly starting to try to make it perform. Everyone knows that lions are wild and savage, although with a trainer they know and respect, they are not. Unfortunately, because horses have the reputation that you can sit on them and kick and they will go and jump and so on, they are taken advantage of and people often never realise just how dangerous they can be.

Even a tiny pony can pull a huge man around the yard without even feeling it. A horse that is not being ridden or looked after properly, flying around like a loaded cannon, is a very dangerous thing. Young horses are especially potentially dangerous because they are only half-grown and half-trained and still very unpredictable, yet so many novices take on youngsters.

'There are so many unhappy owners and unhappy horses around'

I do appreciate that there needs to be respect. I have said this in my books many times – the horse does need to know that you are 'boss' – but that means being kind and firm and earning respect, not browbeating the horse. It is hard for novices to know where to draw this line, and this is where it is crucial for them to have the right kind of guidance.

I should like to see people learning from scratch along much more classical lines, taking on board what is natural for the horse and understanding that each horse is an individual. We need to see far less of the rather 'hard' way of riding that seems to have crept into many of our riding schools. Even though the manuals of the British Horse Society, for example, outline fairly classical principles of riding, when you go for a lesson many qualified instructors actually teach using methods quite stressful for the horse and for a rider with any sensitivity. By this I mean the emphasis, for instance, on 'Leg, leg, leg' and 'Show it you mean business' and 'Ride into your contact'.

My belief is there needs to be a huge shift in attitudes across the conventional training system. Priorities in many riding schools and training establishments are wrong. Working pupils seem to spend a great deal of time sweeping the yard and tidying the muckheap and, in my opinion, nowhere near enough time is spent with the horses themselves observing them, learning about what they are and seeing that they really are comfortable and happy.

There is also far too much emphasis on competing and winning in the horse world. Children are often given ponies as some kind of status symbol in the first place and, because their idols are competition riders, competing is often all they want to do. I am not against competing as such, but I am against it as an end product. When competition is the be-all-and-end-all of someone's life, it can be tragic because often the horse becomes simply the vehicle. Why can't we all just have confidence in ourselves and enjoy our horses for what they are, instead of what they can do for us?

I believe the end product should be your relationship with your horse. The problem with competing just for your own enjoyment,

> **'Horses have so much to offer us...it is amazing how willing they are'**

though, is that people who don't try to win don't get sponsorship. Whenever money enters into things it becomes a difficult situation. I should like to see more attention paid to the welfare of competition horses. That doesn't mean to say that you cannot train a horse to perform to the highest levels – of course you can, the horse is a strong and fast animal and it loves to gallop and jump. All I am trying to say to riders is: 'Don't do it when your horse has a back problem. Don't do it if they are lame. Be more sensitive and be more aware. If the horse feels well and it trusts you, it will try its heart out for you.'

It is simple to tell the difference between a horse that likes and respects its rider and one that doesn't. Some competitors seem to go through horses at a rate of knots, and other big names have ones that last for years, because you know they have been managed sympathetically. Mary King is a good example. She competes very seriously but her horses always look happy and well – not just bursting out of their skins with fitness because they are corned up, but really enjoying themselves, and she has the same horses year after year.

I think things are slowly coming around now there is a growing interest in classical riding and a more holistic approach to health and well-being is becoming fashionable. If we can get people learning about the physiology and psychology it will be better for us and for the horse. Because of our 'superior' intellect we do have to be in charge, because it would not be safe for the horse to be in charge. And if horses were not useful to us they would have been relegated to the status of zoo or meat animals, which would be a much sadder situation.

Horses have so much to offer us. There isn't another animal in the world that can do for us what horses do. It's amazing how willing and friendly they are when you think how little time in the day we spend with them compared, say, to a dog. Imagine the kind of relationship you could have with a horse if you lived with it! We have pure gold in our hands and often we treat it like brass. I know that sounds dramatic, but we could get much more out of our horses because they are certainly willing to give us more. The horse is truly a unique animal.

REPRODUCTION

Reproduction is the *raison d'etre* of all horses in their natural state, whether they be feral mustangs in the Nevada desert or the pampered performance animal in our stable. For those of us who do not breed from our horses, their sexual needs are given little consideration – until they start to cause inconvenient behaviour. An in-season mare causing a stir among the geldings she shares her paddock with, or being reluctant to concentrate on her work is suddenly a nuisance.

As with most mammals, the ability of the mare to conceive a foal depends on the physiological moment being right, and so the strength of the urge to mate ebbs and flows in synch with the state of readiness of her body. In horses this receptive period is short – around five days every three weeks – and also seasonal, dictated by her hormones which are, in turn, activated by the longer daylight hours of the spring and summer months. Behaviour influenced by the drive to mate also varies during the reproductive cycle and according to the time of the year. For the mare there is little point using

sexually-motivated behaviour during the weeks when she is not able to mate successfully anyway. Sexual activity is confined to those days when she is receptive. It focuses on an involved courtship procedure based on a set of very precise communication cues understood by both parties. Without these very specific behavioural prompts, successful mating will not take place. The mare will not accept the stallion, or the stallion will not respond to the mare. He has to learn, through bitter and often uncomfortable experience, to interpret the signs of readiness correctly and well if he is going to avoid serious damage to his health. On the appropriate cue he will react instantly and instinctively with the appropriate physical response, with no conscious deliberation, as does the mare. Stallions are ready and willing to mate at any time that they receive stimuli that they interpret as an ' invitation' from a mare.

As humans are intent on breeding selectively, very few horses except those living a feral lifestyle have the chance to indulge in completely natural patterns of sexual behaviour. Mares enjoy a relatively 'normal' existence, though many establishments will separate them off even from geldings to avoid the squabbles and jealousies that still arise during season times. The same could hardly be said for the vast majority of entire males, most of whom spend most of their lives in virtual solitary confinement – cooped up in a stable to avoid 'anti-social' antics, brought out only for severely restricted exercise on the end of a rope and chain, or, when it is time to serve a mare, the mating takes place with only the most cursory of pre-copulatory introductions. It is these abnormal conditions which all too often produce abnormally aggressive behaviour.

In the natural state preliminaries are precise and involved, but once the stallion is given the green light, mating itself is a brief affair taking much less than a minute. Prolonged copulation would do the horse no favours in the survival business, being somewhat incompatible with sudden swift flight. Equine sexual tactics are therefore based on intense stimulation, followed by immediate release, with no time wasted. By serving the same mare several times over a four- or five-day spell, the stallion maximises the chances of conception.

SOCIAL INTERACTIONS

Herd living makes good survival sense for prey species. Banding together in a group offers security as it greatly reduces the chances of any individual being picked off by predators, while, at the same time, providing an ideal opportunity to find a mate. Reduced danger levels mean more time for eating – and when it comes to searching out food and water, a dozen noses are certainly better than one. A horse's whole mental and behavioural make-up is tailored to community living in this way, and the need for social contact with others of its own kind is one of the strongest of all its built-in urges. True, horses will live by themselves and, once again, it is just as well they are so adaptable, as they are very often forced to do so. A contented, relaxed horse that feels secure will eat, stand and ride out happily on his own, and with training and confidence in his rider, he can show breath-taking courage – blazing around a formidable cross-country course in cold blood

or pushing himself to the limits on an endurance trail. Under pressure, though, the insecure horse will always nap to his companions. Given a choice, any horse, almost without exception, will choose to be with other horses.

Consider what a horse forced to live a solitary life isolated, or even simply separated, from the company of his own kind is missing out on. All the to-ing and fro-ing of equine chit-chat, the squabbles and the escapades, cementing old friendships with a mutual scratching session, avoiding the herd 'bully' here, seeing off old enemies there, taking turns to scout for fresh pasture, watching for danger signals and reacting with a rush of adrenalin and a sprint to the far end of the field, or just the chance to doze for a few moments, secure in the knowledge that someone else is on the look-out. Almost all the satisfying activities and diversions that fill the hours of the free-roaming horse in a social group are denied to a horse living on his own, be it in a paddock or a loose box. No doubt he considers the hour or so a day of human company and conversation we offer a very poor substitute (though it is certainly better than nothing at all). Loneliness is a miserable existence for a horse.

The magnetic drive to band up and interact as a wild herd is illustrated in any domestic situation where horses are grouped together, whether it is out at pasture, a lesson in the manege, a line of trekking ponies or even in a livery yard. Each group is a mirror of the herd in the wild, linked together by a network of friendships,

'Loneliness is a miserable existence for a horse... he craves a sense of belonging, just as we do'

Herd behaviour will develop within any groups of horses that spend time together – in the wild, in the field, in the riding school manege or among the racing string.

hierarchical pressures and, if applicable, family bonds. Every 'team' is likely to be more settled and content if these complex strands of relationship are not being constantly muddled, or the equilibrium shattered by introducing new individuals and taking out others. A settled yard is a far less stressful environment than one whose inmates are constantly coming and going. A horse craves for a sense of 'belonging', just as we do.

STRUCTURE OF THE HERD

The same basic social rules apply in any group of horses and can be seen at their purest in the way that wild or feral communities organise themselves. Here, the herd usually consists of about four to eight individuals, though numbers can be as few as two and as many as twenty or more. The 'team list' of the average herd would consist of one mature stallion, his 'harem' of a handful of mares, and their offspring up to the age of about two years.

THE STALLION: The traditional image of a macho male at the head of the herd, defending his mares ferociously against predators simply does not fit the facts. Studies of feral horse bands have shown that the stallion takes on more of a 'chairman's' role. Everyone knows he is the boss, but he is the hard-working organiser of the group rather than some kind of tyrannical dictator. Whenever the herd moves on, or if danger threatens, the stallion is invariably to be found trailing at the back of the group, neck stretched out snaking and weaving, ears flat, keeping them all together and driving on the stragglers in much the same way as a diligent sheepdog.

Ever-protective, the stallion rarely shows any genuinely aggressive behaviour towards his own band – he saves this for any challenges that might arise from other males approaching, intent on stealing his mares. Fights do then occur, with the defending stallion positioning himself firmly between his mares and the intruder, and then there are no holds barred. If the battle is lost, the newcomer takes over as head of the group and the old ruler is ousted to lead a solitary life. More often, unless the mature stallion is incapacitated in some way, it is the challenger who is driven away.

THE 'BOSS' MARE: Who leads the way if the stallion is generally busy in his 'shepherding' role? Almost every herd has one matriarch, the 'boss mare' or alpha mare who makes all the tough decisions, and who frequently initiates movement of the group and acts as path-finder. She is often the law-enforcer too. If a young colt plays over-rough or begins paying a little too much attention to the females, it is often this matron who sees him off in no uncertain terms.

OTHER MARES: The remaining mares are those with young foals at foot and, possibly a few barren mares who generally help out as "aunties" and with the herding duties.

While foals are still young their mothers are fiercely protective of them. Strong family bonds exist while the offspring remain with the herd, and the 'nuclear family' is the foundation of the group. Maturing youngsters face a changing identity within the band that is sometimes hard to come to terms with.

YOUNG FILLIES: They may stay with the group for up to a year or more after gradual, natural weaning, but their father will not generally mate with them so they are not discouraged from wandering off to join up with a bachelor group of males, or be claimed by another stallion.

YOUNG MALES: They have a tougher time, clearly posing a threat to their sire as they strengthen and mature. From the age of around eighteen months onwards, colts are driven away from the herd and group at a distance into "bachelor" sets. Eventually, a particularly vigorous young stallion might challenge an older male for his harem or, alternatively, begin to force away his bachelor companions and claim any fillies that have joined with them for his own.

Besides the family bonds, what kind of affiliations keep the group together? Horse societies are certainly peaceful communities where harmony is the keynote and there is rarely any serious conflict. Squabbling between band members would be a distraction that would work against the interests of the group as a whole, so it tends to be friendships and affiliations that provide the framework rather than social status. The old idea of the 'pecking order', where each individual group member earns their rung on the hierarchical ladder by challenging and resisting challenge has been shown, through observation, to barely apply

Affiliations are more important to horse society than conflict. Close friends indulge in mutual grooming, allowing each other access to personal space.

to equine societies, especially in the wild. For species that need to compete for a limited supply of food, such as birds, then the old pecking order may be the simplest way of avoiding continual, debilitating battles. Given enough space, however, there is little or no competition between horses for their food, so why fight about it? Dominance hierarchies only tend to emerge within societies where a resource is scarce or under threat. It is rarely seen in wild horses, and is only slightly more significant in domestic groups at feed times for example.

What horses understand is co-operation and getting along. Not naturally dominant or aggressive creatures, they do not go out looking for fights like humans will. The horse is a sociable creature who feels most secure living by clear rules and with a firm lead, especially if he is young or timid by nature.

It is a willingness we should give him more credit for, before presuming, at the slightest hiccup in training, that he is being deliberately antagonistic or awkward. There is no doubt that a less amiable animal would never have allowed mankind to become so intimate with him, or left himself so open to exploitation by another species in so many ways.

This is not to say there is never any conflict within the herd in the wild, or within the herd in your field. As any owner can observe, individuals have their own personalities and some will show themselves to be more, or less, dominant than others. The bullies are not necessarily the leaders of the group though – the field 'thug' is rarely the one who makes all the decisions. Dominance relationships in a horse community are never rigid or static; they continually shift and change according to context. There are sure to be some individuals who will always be the top dogs and some are destined to be the under-dogs, but, more often, in one situation a particular horse might take the dominant role, where in another he could be subordinate. When danger strikes all are equal, acting as one. In addition to dominance relationships, definite likes or dislikes develop, creating a complicated web of affiliations and preferences. Between them all, these influences can pull and tug the herd along, as individuals cling to their special friends and avoid the group members they dislike. Within a free or natural-living group the firmest attachments will be between family members, in particular between mothers and their foals, between brothers and between sisters.

Though domesticated horses rarely have the opportunity to grow up within a multi-age family group, other friendships are struck up which can become extremely strong, ignoring the usual codes of conduct and severely disrupting the 'standard' established status ladder. This can be seen within any group of horses kept together,

'Horses are like humans in needing their own personal space'

and it can sometimes cause real problems when close friends are reluctant to be separated, even for a minute. Every horse will have his preferred companion and another he takes a definite dislike to, and, to us, the choice can appear totally eccentric. Even so, petty jealousies are bound to arise, and certain situations do strain the bonds of friendship to their limits – such as when too few piles of hay are put out in the paddock or someone approaches the group with a bucket. There are plenty of opportunities for us to be more sensitive to our horses' choice of friends and adjust arrangements accordingly, so situations likely to lead to stress or conflict can be avoided. Stabling sworn enemies next door to each other, or even insisting on riding them out together is asking for trouble. Equally, the company of a known friend or leader-type can be reassuring and confidence-boosting in testing situations, such as meeting a frightening new obstacle. So long as the space is large enough and feed is not allowed to become a rivalry issue, what is wrong with accommodating an amicable pair in the same large stable?

The context most likely to upset the applecart of relationships is over-crowding, and the reason for this is two-fold. Firstly, too many horses means demand for basic commodities, such as food, outstrips supply, so immediately a forceful, aggressive hierarchy takes over where individuals are insisting on attention. Secondly, horses are like humans in needing their own personal space to feel comfortable. Every horse appears to have an oval-shaped area extending some two to four metres all around him that he considers his own 'safety zone'. Only intimate friends can expect an unqualified welcome here, and others can expect to be driven away. Beyond this 'bubble', defined by threat-distance, is a larger one that the horse regards as his flight distance. Suspicious intruders venturing into this wider area provoke an escape reaction.

Over-crowding, or threatening a horse's own territory in any way, is as stressful to him as leaving him completely alone. When personal spaces are continually being encroached, stress and anxiety ripples through the group, fraying nerves and putting individuals on edge. In the domesticated situation the horse finds it hard to relax if his safe area might be violated without invitation – from horse or human. Touchy horses will edge away in the field, but in the conventional loosebox that option is closed and the presumptive intruder may get a warning face, or worse, to tell him to watch his step. Dominant, 'bully'-type personalities are far more sensitive about guarding their individual distances, which appear to be more extensive than those of more submissive characters. As a rule, domesticated horses get resigned to us constantly invading their space without asking permission, but the invisible boundaries are easy to see in unhandled or loose animals. Nevertheless, whenever we approach a horse it would still be more polite – and sensible – to hesitate for a moment within the flight boundary to judge whether our presence is being interpreted as an intrusion or not.

Meetings are of intense interest to such social animals and, as we have already seen, they are a time of rapid exchange of signals. Any number of potential outcomes could develop depending on the circumstances, the characters involved and how body language is interpreted. For example, if the stranger is adopting an aggressive-type stance (head-on, eyes staring) it will provoke a different response to a stranger with a submissive pose (angled, eyes averted, in human terms shoulders slightly hunched). When the encounter is a horse-human one, especially when the horse is young or unfamiliar, the wisest policy is to be slightly cautious and let him make the first move.

Horses grazing together will tend to keep their personal distances unless they are special friends but, equally, they will never want to stray too far from other group members either. The braver souls stretch this 'herd distance' further than the worriers, and a happy, relaxed bunch will always spread more than the frightened crowd who bunch together for added security.

MARCY PAVORD'S VIEW

A successful competitor at the highest levels of endurance riding, Marcy Pavord now concentrates on bringing on young horses and on her work as endurance representative on the British Horse Society's Training and Education Committee. She has been accepted on to the FEI panel as an international candidate judge for endurance riding.

I think what a lot of people in the other main disciplines find hard to get their mind around is that endurance riders are firstly horse-lovers and secondly competitors. Our aim is not to win things but to study our horses and build up a relationship with them.

For endurance you want a horse that is enthusiastic, forward-going and keen. He needs to be brave – the sort of horse that wants to know what is around the next corner, and he needs to be tough. The horse must be bright enough to get himself out of trouble, but careful enough not to get himself into trouble on difficult ground. They must be the sort of horse who thinks ahead. If you are showjumping you don't want a horse that anticipates, but in endurance, once the horse is trained, the fact that he anticipates is marvellous. For example, the horse learns to follow markers and will spot a marker before you will.

Endurance horses have got to be willing to cooperate, to be trainable to be handy at doing things like opening gates very quickly. They have not got to mind going first or last, and they must respect you and listen to you – to see you as a friend, because there will often be times when you are in a bunch of horses and you may not want to go at the same speed, so you need a horse that will respond to you rather than thinking about what the other horses are doing. That can be quite difficult and can take them a long time to learn.

If I was looking at a really young horse, I would go for something bold and curious, not shy, wary or timid. The horse has got to like people – some horses definitely like people and others don't. Some will come galloping up to you if you go into the field, wanting to see you – that's the kind of horse you need, not the type who sees you coming and stalks off to the other side and sticks his nose in the hedge. That type would not be very cooperative when you got to the end of a 100-mile ride and then had to say: 'Come on, you can really do this last 25.'

I like horses that look where they are going and don't fall over their feet. They need to think what they are doing. My good mare, Tara, has always been extremely neat and careful, picking her way through things. My personal preference is for mares, even though they can be a bit hormonal sometimes and say 'I'm not in the mood today.' You do get some excellent geldings, but stallions are not always as good as one would think because they are inclined to worry.

If you are going to buy a horse you really do have to like it at first sight. It's no good thinking: 'Oh well, perhaps I'll grow to like this horse.' It has to have very strong appeal. It is important that you can get on with the horse and that your temperament matches their temperament. They have to respect you and want to do it for you, and that takes time to build up. The more time you spend with each other, the more attached to you they get, and endurance riders spend an awful lot of time with their horses just by the very nature of the sport.

The skill and the challenge in endurance riding is knowing your horse and how far you can push him. Some horses, when they get tired either physically or mentally, just stop and say they are not going any more. They will be perfectly okay, so long as you have not gone beyond their own particular safety margin. The trouble with the right sort of horse is that they are so brave they will keep going when they shouldn't, and, of course, that is where the rider's skill comes in. You have got to learn whether your horse has over-extended himself or not, and you have got to know how to get it round a

'The skill and challenge in endurance riding is knowing your horse and how far you can push him'

difficult course where the conditions are worse than expected. In a race situation, some horses are quite happy to tag along and some are natural leaders – mares in particular – because in the herd it is the mares who are the leader figures and stallions are the rounder-uppers. Those kind of boss mares make brilliant endurance horses. But what you do find is that if they are together they can get incredibly jealous of each other because they are such dominant personalities. Horses that are dominant personalities make good long-distance horses.

Those that want to be in front right from the very beginning don't see it as a race. It is just a flight reaction. A Thoroughbred or an Anglo-Arab tends to just run fast, and it is very easy for it to get to the front of the pack. But after a season or two, the horse will have learnt that they are going to be asked to go a long way, and they have learnt about energy conservation. The ones that are good are the dominant ones who still want to go out and be in front.

Horses pick up what is required from the rider as well. The kind of emotions that horses are aware of, they share with humans, such as trust, fear, confidence. Horses are terribly aware of how humans are feeling at any given time. They must respect their rider enough to listen to them. If you are saying 'Hang on a minute, you can't go that fast,' they have got to have the sense to listen and slow down and stay in balance – and that is where basic training is so important.

SPEAKING THE LANGUAGE

Horses have an extremely sophisticated language of their own. If we are sensitive and experienced enough to learn to interpret it, we can tune in to the equine wavelength and gain a whole new appreciation of the kind of animals they are, and what sort of feelings they have. Equine communication is not based on speech and sound like the human's, and so it is not so adept at conveying precise meaning. However, it is brilliantly effective at expressing shades of mood and communicating emotional statements of infinite subtlety and complexity in just a fraction of a second. How could horse society function without language of some kind? Unless there are forms of communication that every animal in the herd knows and understands, the group would disintegrate into individual units and all the benefits of social living would be lost. 'Horse' is an evolved language, universal to all equines, whether the speaker be a Shetland or a Shire, and the listener a zebra or a Derby winner. As it not our own native tongue, we have to translate the meaning by carefully watching a signal together with the response it elicits.

Messages are sent between horses by cues in their behaviour. Some seem to be innate or inborn, and others appear to have to be learned by the young horse. Some reactions are involuntary and some are quite deliberate. Some convey a definite instruction and others express a general feeling. Some are easy for us to understand, while others require careful study and experience of many horse encounters to guess at with any degree of certainty. Whatever the circumstances, there is no doubt that in any exchange there is far more going on than we 'foreigners' can detect. A whole kaleidoscope of signals converge to create a message – these include smell, taste and touch stimuli and, more obvious to us, statements directed at the ears and the eyes.

Communication goes on constantly, not only between horses but between horses and ourselves. If only we could become as sensitive to the horse's language as he is to the one we teach him, which we expect him to understand despite our vagueness and inconsistency! Horses appreciate it when we do understand what they are saying and show we do by giving the correct response. However poor we are at understanding, they always keep trying to get the message across, even when they know – as older and wiser horses do – how bad we are at it. The time when we really need to worry about a horse is when he switches off and abandons his attempts to communicate at all.

MONTY ROBERTS' VIEW

Monty Roberts has stunned audiences worldwide with demonstrations of his 'advance and retreat' method of starting young horses. Appalled by the brutality of conventional cowboy techniques, which aimed literally to break the horse in body and spirit, Roberts spent years observing the behaviour of the feral mustangs of Nevada and Idaho, which he describes as "raw pure minds". His approach aims to win the animal's trust and confidence by communicating in its own language – the language of body stance and gesture. The result is the ability to bring a totally untouched youngster to the point of following him around as if on some invisible leadrope (a phenomenon he terms 'join-up'), being happily tacked up and ridden away in a remarkably short space of time.

People ask me how this system works in thirty minutes compared to the usual six weeks. It is because it is cheating. It taps in to the communication system of the horse, which makes the whole business a whole lot easier. I have the horse's permission to do whatever I do. The

horse is talking to me, and I am understanding what he is saying. The language is predictable, it is discernible and it is effective – in my demonstrations I set out to show these three things. The language is also universal – all horses understand it – among themselves, they do not need interpreters. They are 65 million years old and they are all spawned from one area, so they have had a lot longer than us to create a system of communication. My confidence comes from the fact that the horses respond. It is not my language, it is theirs. I speak volumes to them, but not in English or any audible language, because their language is not audible.

When I turn the horse loose in the round pen he is a flight animal, I am a fight animal, so he leaves. I say to him, 'Whatever you want to do is okay – if you want to go, go, but you have to work for it.' He will still believe I don't speak his language, because he's never come across a human being before that does. But I'll be saying 'Go' with my shoulders square and my eyes pinned on him. When he doesn't want to go any more, he will ask to renegotiate the contract, first by opening up the ear closest to me, then probably by coming off the fence and trying to get closer to me.

After that there are two pieces of communication open to him before I am satisfied that he wants to be with me. One is licking and chewing – that says, he's a herbivore, a flight animal, but he doesn't believe I'm going to hurt him so he's continuing to eat. Horses are constantly in fear of their own lives and most of the time we add to that fear. We don't help them at all. Generally the last thing they do is drop the head down near the sand. That says, 'If we can renegotiate, I'd like to be chairman please. I'd like to bring the agenda.' After

RIGHT: *"I am setting up a bargain with the horse that I am not going to hurt him... I am going to offer him a safety zone, so when he is a good boy everything is right, there is a positive consequence for positive action...but he must be responsible for his own actions." Monty Roberts working a youngster in the round pen.*

BELOW: *"The foremost principle is to get the horse on your side – to find common ground." Richard Maxwell, who trained with Monty Roberts, uses the 'advance and retreat' method to start young horses and overcome remedial problems. Here he demonstrates 'join-up'.*

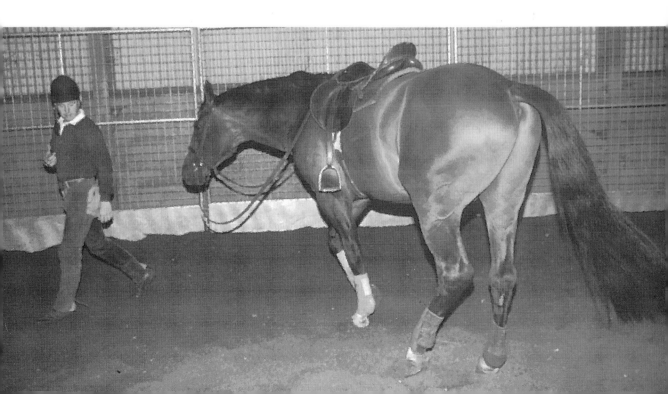

that, I go passive, avert the eyes, bring myself in front of the horse, bring my near shoulder back past its head and invite the horse towards me.

What I am doing is mimicking the language between a more dominant horse to a horse lower down the social ladder. I learned this from watching the lead mare in a herd schooling the other horses – she was my teacher. Each wild horse herd had one essential teacher and that was always a mare. She told those kids what to do all day long, she told the stallion what to do, she said what the herd was going to eat and what direction they were going to travel. Having said that, I am not looking for submission. I am looking for a 50-50 partnership where the horse isn't one step lower or higher than me. Later on then, if obstacles outside the human race become obstacles to learning, you must become the safety zone. If you use force you will only keep him away.

My method was a response to the way I saw horses being treated on the ranches, which is very extreme. The intention with my method is to deal with the horse with absolutely no pain. I'm pretty darn stringent about that. I am for whipless racing, but that is not because I'm a bleeding heart and I think the poor little horse is going to die of the hurt. I believe pain is a bad tool. After about four races, if you sting a horse with that whip enough, he literally runs slower than he does when you don't. He starts to resent it, to the extent that when you pressure him in a race he thinks he's going to get hit so he backs up. So I don't hit horses.

'I don't talk to horses, I listen to them, and through that listening they listen to me'

I am not saying that a good horse cannot be made any other way. It can be 'started' my way or it could be done carefully in the more conventional English way. The two methods start off apart but as you take a horse through its disciplines both come closer and closer together. Good horsemen will make champions, and there have been champions for hundreds of years that I have never touched. What I am trying to say is that more horses will have a chance this way. You can do it better, so that the horse never suffers restraint or pain, and it really works. You don't ever have to believe 'I have got to hurt him so he knows who's boss.'

That horse will try harder for you if you don't and I can prove it. Horses get precious little reward for the good things they do in life, so the more we try to reward them the better they will be. If a horse is started off right you should never have to use discipline at all.

What it hinges on is giving an alternative. You have got to give the man an alternative and the horse an alternative: that he can lead a much more comfortable life and be happier doing it this way. If you haven't set up the environment where that can happen, you have made a mistake. What you are doing then is ending up reinforcing negative behaviour by fighting about it. It is no different from a marriage or a family, from disputes between a mother and daughter, or father and son. If all you do is fight about it, it will just stay that way. You get an alternative going – 'Okay, if we don't fight what else are we going to do?' – and then you have a chance to lead a more reasonable life.

When we are starting a horse, or even sorting out a remedial problem, what I hope to set up is an agreement that the horse himself will cause something to happen or not happen. I am setting up a bargain with him that I am not going to hurt him. I am not going to do anything but offer up a consequence for negative action. Then I am going to offer him a safety zone, so when he is a good boy I tell him how nice he is, that everything is right, that there is a positive consequence for positive action. But everything he chooses to do that is outside the parameters of the respect I ask of him, that will cost him. So he understands very quickly what is the good part. I am here to give the horse a chance to fail and a chance to succeed. But he must be responsible for his own actions.

All the young baby horses I start come to me pure, with their soft under-bellies exposed, every single one of them. They don't come to me with problems. Someone, at some point, has the responsibility of that horse's future. In the cases of those that come for remedial work that responsiblity has been failed to a great extent. It is my strong opinion that a good trainer can hear a horse speak to him – a great trainer can hear a horse whisper. A lot of the remedial horses I see aren't whispering or talking or even shouting – they're screaming and hollering and pounding the floor, and still some trainers wouldn't hear. Or, they would choose to ignore it.

There are only two types of people I cannot teach this to. One is the person who is frightened of horses and who is afraid to get around a horse. My pulse rate is always low and I never allow myself to become tense, whatever situation might occur. The other person I cannot teach this to is the person who doesn't believe it will work. If you don't believe it will work, the horse will know it and he will block you off.

I don't talk to horses, I listen to them and through that listening they listen to me. But the conversation always starts the other way around – I have to hear them before they can hear me. All I aim to do is to create an environment where they can learn, where instead of trying to push knowledge in, I can just stand back, be the spectator, watch them learn and marvel at how they have been able to teach me their language.

THE HORSE'S VOCAL REPERTOIRE

Compared to a species which relies so heavily on audible language like ourselves, the horse' s repertoire of communicative sounds is small, but, nonetheless, it is still useful. Unlike human vocalisation, horse calls tend to convey more about the general mood of the horse than set, specific meanings, which will vary according to the total situation. The main sounds, with their typical messages are:

NEIGH OR WHINNY: The longest and loudest call, made with the mouth open and usually answered by another horse if there is one within ear-shot. It is a "Hello, I'm over here, are you out there somewhere?" appeal, and the response tells the caller: "Yes, okay, I can hear you." These neighs help horses contact and locate other group members at a distance, and all have an individual quality that others soon learn to recognise and use for identification purposes. There is no anxiety or alarm in a neigh, which is an information-seeking call.

SNORT: This forceful exhalation through the nostrils carries a double-edged message of alarm: "There's something here that could be dangerous – get ready for flight." A snorting horse dilates his nostrils and takes in deep breaths, opening up his respiratory system and absorbing oxygen to ready his muscles for action. The noise alerts other horses both to the possibility of danger and the direction it is coming from.

NICKER: There are several variations on this low-pitched, pulsating sound. One is most definitely a "Hello, pleased to see you, do come along" welcome, used at fairly close quarters to an equine friend or, often, a human one who might be bringing food. Stallions use a longer, deeper and more pulsating greeting nicker to a mare who has really caught their fancy, usually bobbing the head up and down simultaneously. The equivalent of anxious human whispering, the mare's soft maternal nicker to her foal is barely audible, and tells him she is concerned, so please stay closer.

BLOW: Like a short, powerful snort without the vibrations or the accompanying tension. The message can be one of curiosity: "Huhh! What's this?" – or simply a spirited statement that the caller is feeling good.

SQUEAL: "Watch it!" This is a close-range warning or indignant protest, to be ignored at peril, unless the encounter is a sexual one, in which case the mare might be up to her share of teasing. Squeals can be short or long but are usually loud – the most serious can be heard some 100 metres away.

ROAR: A fierce, raw noise or high-pitched scream, seldom provoked in domestic situations but to be heard in the wild when emotions of anger or fear are running high.

Other sounds are not intended to convey any particular meaning, such as the grunts and groans occasionally heard during extreme exertion or pain, or when a horse is getting up from the ground or having a yawn. Equine sighs tend to indicate boredom or being fed-up, just like our own. A hearty nose blow is a good sign of general contentment with life, though a sharper sneeze has a slight expectant, edgy quality.

BODY TALK

The outline and attitude of the horse's body speaks volumes to his companions about his mood and the state of his emotions. Each horse watches the others continually for visual communication in this way. Every part of the body contributes to the overall picture and adds nuances of meaning to the general impression. As a rule, the more taut, agitated and elevated the body outline, the more excited the horse is, and the lower and droopier the posture, the more dozy, submissive or dejected. In the middle lie any number of degrees of feeling somewhere between the two.

Everything about the alarmed or aroused horse is tense, and vertical, demanding attention, crying out to be noticed. A startled horse that has spotted something intensely interesting or alarming is a perfect example. The body presents an outline of curves and angles which provokes excitement and alertness in other horses, and eye-catching prancing, jerky steps reinforce this signal. Only when escape is underway does the sheer exertion of moving at full speed flatten the outline again. Body stiffness and abrupt, tense or nervous movements mean one thing, and one thing only, to a horse – danger.

Interpreting and acting on the slightest of alarm signals has been crucial to the horse's survival, so it is a well-practised skill and

Everything about the excited horse is 'up' and tense – a powerful and comprehensive signal to others, and one that is highly infectious.

almost a reflex reaction. It comes as no surprise then that warning bells are set ringing by any signs of body tension they see in us, because horses are as clever at understanding our body language and 'catching' our moods as they are their own. So often a breakdown in communication leads to problems when a rider or handler fails to realise this, or does not interpret equine body language correctly, even when it is being positively shouted at them. A horse that becomes edgy and on his toes with a nervous novice is less likely to be plotting to take advantage of the human's lack of expertise than rapidly being overcome with fright, thinking: "Help, if he's worried then there must be something to worry about – I'm off!" A fearful horse goes almost rigid, especially in his mouth and neck. He cannot

relax, can no longer feel the bit or any of his rider's aids, and often will not go forwards until the tension has been released from his body. At the opposite extreme, relaxed muscle tone, a saggy, smooth outline and slow, unhurried movements have a soothing effect on other horses – there is nothing worthy of interest or effort going on. The head is low, tail tucked in, a foot might be resting and the whole body image becomes smaller and lower to the ground. Likewise a human who is at ease, moving carefully, openly and confidently, inspires security and reassurance in the horse.

Certain specific whole-body movements signal particular meanings and tend to be display threats aimed at reinforcing status or settling disputes, without having to resort to an actual fight and potential injury. By a

'Interpreting and acting on the slightest of alarm signals has been crucial to the horse's survival'

ABOVE: Action! The flight instinct is so reflexive it takes long and patient training to over-ride. Every muscle of this alarmed horse is tense, ready for positive exertion.

RIGHT: Any kind of restraint can potentially panic an insecure or untrained horse, whose freedom is his life.

body check, a dominant horse will swing around in front of a rival, blocking his advance. The other horse is then forced to decide between either a direct challenge or backing down by turning away. Sometimes the body check is carried one step further, into an intimidating shoulder barge that actually makes contact with the other horse. Polo ponies are actually encouraged to barge in this way to see off a tackle, and race jockeys are severely penalised if they are seen to resort to bumping rivals with this physically and psychologically off-putting tactic.

If the threat of action can have the desired effect, it is usually preferred to all-out confrontation. So a horse that is prepared to kick out in defence often swings his rump around in readiness, indicating to others: "Get out of my way, or else!" This warning sign is generally taken seriously and avoids a nasty showdown. Rear-end-on threats are almost always defensive in nature and based on fear, the horse's aim being to fight off real or potential attack. True aggression takes the form of an angry front-on assault which is fortunately – and interestingly – rarely used against humans. Both aggressive and defensive reactions consist of a series of related signals of intent that rapidly increase in intensity until the threat is acted on: "I' m warning you...right...take that!"

When the losing combatant wants to submit, he turns away and throws in the towel – his victor rarely goes 'in for the kill', he is usually grateful to have escaped injury in the conflict himself. A research study that observed 1,162 disputes at a watering place found that in 76 per cent of cases the individuals did not come to blows because the disagreement never got beyond the threat stage. There we have an intelligent animal.

TOPS AND TAILS

The ears and the tail are both superb signallers and often work in tandem. They are so effective because both are so conspicuous and alter the all-important body outline so dramatically. A high tail equals exuberance. Highest of all is the flagged tail of a stallion courting or facing challenge, of an interesting meeting, a good game or the sprint to escape. At these times the tail can even be arched right back over the quarters. Still aroused but at less of an angle, is the tail of a horse excited or threatened by an encounter of some kind, on the alert, or a sexually-displaying mare. The tail is always raised slightly during movement, the faster or more active the pace, the greater the lift. A low tail indicates a horse is either relaxed and sleepy or possibly feeling discomfort. Flattened against the rump the tail shows a horse who is afraid, either in a submissive way or in fear of attack, during a chase, or readying for defence. Swishing or lashing the tail has meaning too – generally that something is annoying or frustrating the horse, provoking the same kind of reaction as that triggered by an irritating fly. Physical pain can be behind a lashing tail, but anger and conflict are also shown this way, and in a dressage test it is marked down as a display of resistance. At the other end of the body, ears also rise and fall with interest and arousal.

> *'The ears and the tail are both superb signallers and often work in tandem'*

73

Neutral ears sit slightly forwards in the best position for all-round coverage. When the ears are alerted they will point in the direction of the horse's attention, and their angle indicates the level of concentration. So the harder they are pricked forwards, the more intense the interest forwards. One or both ears can be held sideways or half backwards to tune in on activity from the side or rear, and ears go back to focus on sounds from behind. One might go one way and one another, perhaps still or perhaps flicking to and fro, indicating either split attention or anxious uncertainty. The ears' job as signal receivers can over-ride and interfere momentarily with their other role as communicators, so both horses and humans need to learn to differentiate at a glance the times when they are indicating attention to sound and the times when they are displaying emotion.

Floppy ears illustrate a relaxed state, doziness or lethargy, though very drooping ears are completely turned off, indicating pain, depression or submission. More extreme fear or submission shows in ears held tensely backwards. Pressed flat against the head the ears are protected – usually from big trouble of some kind that the horse is about to be either on the receiving end of or about to dish out.

MAKING FACES

Horses may not be able to achieve the range of expression that the human face can call on, but movements and tensions, especially in the mouth and nose areas, can convey both dramatic and detailed statements. When lips are drawn back exposing the teeth, a definite message is being sent, though it is not necessarily always one of open-mouthed aggression. The submissive opening and closing movement of the young foal 'snapping' tells the receiver of the signal – usually a large adult – "Please don't hurt me, I'm only little. Look, I still suckle...". As foals mature and grow in confidence and status within the herd they lose this reaction. The other dramatic mouth movement is flehmen, used by the stallion to smell the urine of a mare, or occasionally by other horses when they encounter a strange taste or odour.

More subtle but equally meaningful is the degree of stiffness or relaxation of the mouth and muzzle. As always, tension equals stress – conflict, fear, alarm, anger. The lips are fastened down tightly over the teeth, elongating the nose and the jaw is fixed so that the chin hardens into a ball. Taut, flared nostrils produce a 'triangle of stress' above the mouth. In contrast, a relaxed, unstressed or exhausted horse has a drooping, sagging mouth, and a nose with very loose muscle tone. Noses can lengthen at other times too, not only when the horse is under pressure. A long nose with a relaxed mouth indicates curiosity and playfulness, or, if it is jiggling about, it may be offering an invitation to come close for a mutual grooming session, or indicate an urge to scratch or to go in search of something in your pocket. Noses can wrinkle up in irritation, disgust or discomfort, or when a mare is mated. Nostrils flared to take in maximum air always signify a state of intense emotion. Moving up the head, the eyes are understandably opened wide with apprehension or alertness but more or less closed with relaxation, submission or fatigue. Anger shows with the rolling back and bulging of the eye, though it is not true to say that a horse showing the whites of its eyes is always ill-tempered. Most likely he is simply trying to focus on something going on behind him.

Fear shows itself in the high heads, flattened ears, rolling eyes and tense muscles of these youngsters at a sale.

BY A HEAD

Most obvious and common of all head movements in herd-living horses is the shovelling upward jerk of the head thrust, generally accompanied by an open mouth and pressed-back ears to indicate a business-like "Watch it!" If the warning is not heeded a body lunge or even charge could follow through the threat. Less assertive is the gentler nudge with ears at half-cock or forwards. This says: "Hey, I'm here" or "Come on then, what are we waiting for?' – it demands attention. Shaking or tossing of the head invariably shows degrees of annoyance and can become a habit that persists long after the original cause has

been removed. The origin of the movement, way back in evolution, would have been to rid the animal of biting insects, but nowadays the source of the irritation could be anything from a fly to unwanted restraint, badly-fitted tack or the clumsy hands of the rider.

A cocky show-off might display the slow side-to-side nose shake that says: "I'm mighty pleased with myself." Ducking the head up and down repeatedly, coupled with alert eyes and ears, shows the horse attempting to figure out and focus on an unfamiliar object some way away. A frightened animal may jerk backwards abruptly, pulling away rapidly from the source of his alarm, whether it is a threatening horse or a threatening handler. A step beyond this becomes a rear, and then the handler could have a real problem.

The horse's long, strong and flexible neck works in conjunction with the head to turn it and help orientate the senses on a particular stimulus. The neck also delivers its own independent communication messages. A startled or aroused horse will swell its muscles with the neck becoming taut and elevated. Swinging the neck away from something signals the wish to avoid an unpleasantness. A herding stallion will lower his head, step high and stretch out his neck, snaking it from side-to-side with a curious rhythmic, darting action that probably initiated as a series of bite-threats, but has now been generalised into this distinctive "move-along" chase command. This is quite different to neck-wringing, a curious contorting twisting of the head and neck. This happens in play, but at other times it is a sign of stress and frustration. This could apply to a troubled horse who, perhaps, wants to act aggressively but cannot bring himself to take the plunge and would rather not be in the situation he finds himself.

LEGGING IT
Besides the general impression conveyed by

Foreleg strike aggression is a warning in no uncertain terms.

the movement itself – jerky and high-stepping or slow and lackadaisical – more specific individual leg movements carry their own meaning. Any kind of stamping action is generally a kind of mild protest and is a modified form of kicking. A horse will stamp at annoying flies he cannot get rid of, or at having his girth tightened, or a mare might object to the persistent, unwanted attentions of her foal. Scraping and pawing the ground has the purely functional purpose of investigating the terrain underfoot, preparing a patch for rolling or pushing away ice or snow. But the horse that paws the ground because he is keen to get moving, or cannot get to his feed bucket is showing impatience and thwarted desire to reach something.

A front leg lifted during feeding is most likely to be simply a mild form of pawing, but a sharply raised foot denotes a first warning: "I could strike you...". The rapid forward flick of the foreleg that is a proper strike is an amplification of this, often seen at a meeting between strangers. It may be accompanied by an indignant squeal – "Oi, keep your distance!"

Full-blooded strikes with both forelegs are part of the fighting stallion's armoury. Likewise, at the rear end, lifting or waving a hind leg is hinting that a horse is weighing up his target, and if provoked any further might let fly in earnest with one or both barrels. It is often used to back up the rump presentation message if that has failed as a deterrent.

4 *HOW DO HORSES LEARN?*

If the horse's behaviour patterns were not as perfectly evolved to suit his lifestyle as his body, he would most certainly not have made it this far. What equine mentality is perfectly adapted to is the natural environment of a horse, not of a man. So when we attempt to make valuations about the horse's mental scope, his intelligence and the way he learns, we have to remember that comparisons with ourselves – or any other animal – have very little meaning. In his own surroundings the horse is supreme, every action and reaction fine-tuned, extremely sensible and suitable. In the surroundings we expect him to live and perform in, a large proportion of those in-built reactions are totally inappropriate – and therefore, not surprisingly, they are labelled clumsy, senseless or stupid.

As we have already seen, there is a ground-plan for the physical horse that provides for the structure and framework of a superbly adapted flight animal. But what about a psychological blueprint? How does his mind operate?

A MENTAL BLUEPRINT
There is much still to be learned about the workings of the brain, both human and equine, but as both are basically the same in structure, it is reasonable to assume that they function in much the same way. It is known that different areas of the brain are associated with different 'jobs' and act as control panels for these functions.

The large frontal area of the brain, the cortex, is usually associated with conscious thought and learning. It analyses visual and auditory input, and governs the sense of touch and voluntary movements. Also believed to be located in the cortex is the functioning of the personality and its integration with the body and behaviour. At the very front of this area the olfactory lobes deal with the closely-related senses of smell and taste. The cerebral cortex is split, as in the human brain, into left and right hemispheres, each dealing only with messages coming from its opposite side. Compared to the way our own brain functions, however, the horse has only a limited ability to cross-refer between hemispheres. As a result, every lesson the horse is expected to learn needs to be taught equally thoroughly from both sides. Working evenly on both reins and handling from the near and off sides is important for physical development – but it is equally significant in terms of mental balance. If a task is always carried out on one side only, the horse can react as if he has never experienced it before when it is attempted on the other. Likewise, a bad encounter associated particularly with the left side, for example, could produce a fear reaction if it is experienced again on that side but no response at all – at first, at any rate – if it appears on the right.

The horse has a very large cortex, which ought to give us some indication of his capacity for learning and his reasoning power. It is thought that the more convoluted the cortex, the more intelligent the animal, which would place the horse far in advance of the dog and even on a par with human beings. However, size is also believed to be significant, and for its body volume the horse has a relatively modest brain. So, the theory goes, it is likely to be needing all those convolutions in the cortex just to stay alive and has very little space to spare for the luxury of reasoning, problem-solving and creative thought. Even so, the equine cortex is exceptional, and its size and complexity begs the question: how much do we really understand about what is going on in there and what its potential is? One area that is indisputedly well-developed in equines compared to other species is the hind-brain or cerebellum. This is to be expected in a flight species as it is the main control centre for locomotion, balance and co-ordination of the muscles and limbs. Particular cells (called cristae) register head movement and others (maculae) head position, and so any tilting or restriction on the horse's head will change the way these cells fire their signals to the brain and so affect co-ordination and balance. Tucked in at the back of the hind-brain the medulla regulates vital and involuntary bodily functions such as breathing, swallowing, digestion and the beating of the heart.

In the mid-brain, various areas monitor feeding and temperature control and links between the body and brain. Some reproductive behaviour is controlled here too, but principally the mid-brain is the horse's emotional centre. Deep in the centre an extensive ring-shaped cluster of nerve cells, the limbic system, plays a role in the automatic regulation of body maintenance functions, together with the sense of smell and the emotions. Damage to this area is known to cause abnormal behaviour in humans and in animals.

Interestingly, the proportion of the brain given over to 'feelings' in the horse is just as large as it is in the human, suggesting that horses are capable of feeling a range and depth of emotion as strong as our own – even though their feelings might be inspired by very different situations and triggers. As the equine's 'thinking centre' is less proportionally well-developed, though, it seems to follow that although horses have strong emotions, they do not have much capacity to analyse them. Horses live for the moment and do not waste cerebral energy rationalising their feelings.

The pituitary gland is attached to the base of the brain by a short stalk. This vital gland acts rather like the conductor of the orchestra of hormones which regulate body maintenance and sexual functions and also copes with stress. Another nearby gland, the hypothalmus, registers hunger and thirst and affects the working of the pituitary.

'Although horses have strong emotions, they do not have much capacity to analyse them'

Although parts of the brain have localised functions, they are so closely linked that, effectively, it works as a whole. The animal's physical being is virtually inseparable from its emotions and its intellect, and any disruptions to the functioning of one capacity will undoubtedly cause significant reverberations in other areas.

MEMORY

The memory is the 'hard disc' of the brain computer, recording past experiences and the outcomes of previous choices to use as reference points on which to base future decisions. It is not known where in the brain, human or equine, the memory process takes place as there seems to be no set location, though disturbances in certain areas can cause memory disruption. Also as yet unexplained are the mechanics of memory storage. Different theories suggest that 'spare DNA' in the brain cells is utilised, or that electrical currents within the brain hold the key.

Memory has three stages — registration, storage and recall. In the first stage data is perceived, understood and then slotted in to the short-term memory. The problem with the short-term memory is that it only has a very limited capacity, so unless its contents are continually reconfirmed by constant repetition, they are likely to be replaced by other more pressing information. Data that is important or well-established enough can be transferred to the long-term memory. In the final stage of memory, material is retrieved by being deliberately recalled from the unconscious into the conscious mind.

How reliable and effective the recall system is depends on how well the data was encoded during the storage stage.

As ability to remember is generally considered a sign of high intelligence, horses should fare well in the IQ stakes. Although it is difficult to quantify, they do seem to possess an exceptionally long and clear memory for material that has been effectively stored. It is well known that they will recognise places, other horses and even people after considerable lengths of time, and all trainers are aware that a lesson once thoroughly learnt will 'stick' for years and years without the need to 'top it up' repeatedly. A super-efficient memory evolved as part of a horse's survival mechanism as surely as his limbs and senses. The young horse needs to learn and learn quickly, once and for all, what situations pose a threat, because a prey animal has no room for rehearsals. Knowing where predators were likely to be lurking was a life and death necessity. Remembering from season to season where the waterholes or shelter in a particular territory were located and where rival herds roamed was crucial. Learning which plants tasted good and which didn't, which hurt or which could poison, was of little use if the information could not be retained in the memory and the correct reaction made when the plant was encountered again during the following year's growth cycle.

The horse's talent for remembering places and locations is renowned and is thought to be one of several faculties utilised in their homing ability. In the wild state, after all,

'*A super-efficient memory evolved as part of a horse's survival mechanism as surely as his limbs*'

The horse's powerful memory can work for and against us. Bad memories, involving trauma, stick rapidly and thoroughly. This episode will have done absolutely nothing for the horse's confidence in loading and travelling.

every herd member needed to recall details not only about the landscape of a territory but also areas of difficult terrain perfectly, and recall those details from winter to winter or summer to summer, or however long was necessary. This superb memory brings obvious advantages when it comes to training, but can equally cause problems. Once well-stored, an experience is registered quite possibly for a lifetime, whether it is good or bad. Incorrect training, abuse or uncomfortable experiences – the vet giving an injection, a distressing trip in the trailer, a jab in the mouth over a jump – all will cause an understandable reluctance on the horse's part to expose himself to the chance of possible repetition.

One mistake or bad experience need not spell total disaster, however. Most memories do not become 'permanent' unless they are reinforced by repetition that follows the initial experience very closely, in fact almost immediately. A movement can be taught, but must be repeated several times, straight away, before it can be considered fixed. Likewise, we cannot teach something new, see the horse get it right once and then expect it to remember and repeat the movement correctly weeks, days, or even hours later.

A mistake in training need not become fixed as long as it is not repeated immediately, as it may not have gone beyond the short-term memory. This gives us room to manoeuvre, but it does not let us off the hook completely! Very bad memories, especially those associated with pain or fear, can become instantly fixed if they are dramatic enough or significantly affect the horse himself and his survival. An example would be a traffic accident or even an encounter with a vicious dog at a particular place, or a fall at a certain type of fence. Unpleasant memories can be overcome by patient and consistent re-training and the re-building of trust and confidence, but in many horses this is a long process with no guarantees. Often the old reaction will resurface if an animal is put under stress or pressure.

Learning ability depends to a large extent on how well a memory becomes fixed in the long-term storage bank and how easily the horse can retrieve it. This is affected by several factors. The degree of importance of an experience to the horse is one. Other experiences immediately following the original one that provide associations and reminders are another, and the period of time lapsed before repetition is also significant. When it comes to recall, the particular circumstances, priorities and reminders present at that moment will have a bearing on what information is retrieved and how easily – in other words, what distractions there are and how focused the attention is on the recall request.

TYPES OF BEHAVIOUR

All behaviour falls within two categories. There are species-characteristic activities,

'A great deal of training is designed to dilute or overcome reflex responses'

shown by all members of a species. Then there is individual-characteristic behaviour, which varies from one individual to another. Within each, some fundamental processes are at work which form the basis of the animal's mental make-up.

REFLEXES

These are the simplest behavioural pattern, consisting of high-speed, automatic, unconscious responses of a muscle or a gland to an external stimulus. The reaction is immediate, short-lived and very specific, such as the flick of a muscle to dislodge a fly, the blink of the eye in sudden bright light, or a cough or sneeze on some irritation of the respiratory tract. A network of reflexes control body movement, making sure the right sets of muscles are all synchronising to keep the horse on its feet and produce the different paces. Most reflexes occur with very little involvement by the brain or its memory. A message is picked up by the senses, carried to the spinal column and acted on, without ever needing analysis in the brain itself. This rapid-reaction technique saves precious micro-seconds in a crisis situation. If a horse catches a tiny movement behind him out of the corner of one eye he starts – he does not stay around and take a chance.

That is not to say that the brain has no control at all over reflex actions, some of which can be weakened or even over-ridden by deliberate, cerebral commands. A great deal of training is designed to dilute or overcome reflex responses in this way – such as convincing the horse that any slight movement in his lateral vision is not necessarily a lion skulking in the undergrowth. Reflexes can be dulled, temporarily, too. Repetition of the stimulus that provokes them seems to raise the tolerance threshold, producing a weaker and weaker response.

MAKING CHOICES

Most other behaviour is the result of conscious decision-making on the part of the brain. Data is in-putted – either in the form of a sensory stimulus, an environmental cue, a behavioural signal in another horse, or another kind of message such as an internal signal, perhaps feelings of hunger and thirst or an urge to do something ('motivation').

When a stimulus is received, the brain goes about rapidly processing all the information coming in at that moment, not only sorting it out into priorities but also analysing it in the light of past experiences (learning) stored in its memory. A decision is made based on all the current data available to it. The brain then orders a reaction, which could be in the form of a physical or a behavioural response, or a feeling in the horse. A feeling might be pain or it might be more abstract – fear, anger, maternal 'love', jealousy, etc. Emotions can then become the basis for further motivation: the desire to do a certain thing instead of another. This in itself becomes a stimulus sent back to the brain, and so a cycle can be set up which accelerates (or hinders) learning.

Subjected to this blanketing bombardment, the brain clearly has to filter out some stimuli and sort them into priorities according to its own survival needs. In this way unimportant stimuli never reach the conscious part of the brain to distract or clutter it with unnecessary information. This prioritising builds up to form the horse's perspective on the world around it, and different priorities lead to different species' perception of their surroundings.

How does the sorting take place? On one level, stimuli are sorted by the limitations of the range of the senses themselves – horses can smell things we cannot, for example. Then, once a message is received in the brain, the area dealing with that stimulus can sieve through which signals should be taken notice of and which can be ignored. So a horse can hear all kinds of noises going on but will be most likely to react to another horse call, or to a rustling sound that could indicate danger. Finally, even that filtered data can be over-ridden or switched off, depending on what is happening at that moment and if the brain considers something else to be more crucial – that is, if its attention is focused on another stronger impulse which is given greater priority. So, a terrified horse bent on escape is not interested in the grass beneath his feet, however lush it is or hungry he feels.

Confusion occurs when the horse is caught between two conflicting priorities that have been given equal weighting by the brain. 'Should I go and get a closer look at that strange object in the hedge or should I be running away from it?' 'There's a friend coming down the road – but, then again, here comes my dinner.' 'I want to get to the horse on the other side of the stream, but I

'Personality has a great deal to do with how a horse copes with stressful situations involving choice'

dare not cross the water.' A horse that cannot quite make his mind up, just like a person, becomes stressed and the result is usually one very agitated animal. If the choice is between two conflicting urges, such as moving towards an object or away from it, this is especially difficult, particularly when one possibility is artificially closed such as for a horse in a stable, both scared and fascinated, but with no real escape option. In these circumstances you will often find the erratic, seemingly irrelevant behaviour displayed that is termed 'displacement activity' – such as nervous, frantic snatching at the haynet, or biting at its sides or rugs.

When the horse is prevented from resolving a conflict this can lead to an aggressive reaction too, purely as a result of his frustration – a stallion that smells a receptive mare but is confined to his stable box; a horse that is not given his feed when all the others in the yard are having theirs, banging away on his stable door. Low tolerance to frustration in individuals can lead to abnormal behaviour patterns being set up to provide relief from the conflict – stereotyped stable vices, for example, or a depraved appetite.

Personality has a great deal to do with how a horse can cope with stressful situations involving choice. Does he fly or does he fight? Most often the choice will depend on the circumstances – a startling movement, for instance, is most likely to make the majority of horses run rather than kick. A horse caught up against a fence by a barking dog is more likely to kick as a first reaction than to try jumping the fence. In some situations, however, either could

'From the minute a foal arrives in the world he starts to learn'

happen, and the horse's first choice depends very much on him and his own past experiences. As both reactions are fuelled by adrenalin, he can switch between one and the other at the speed of a thought.

STRATEGIES

Stimuli and experiences are given priority ratings that influence the horse's reaction. But how are the ratings allocated in the first place? What decides what those priorities should be for an equine – which, after all, are totally different to the priority 'rating' for a human being, a polar bear or a rhinoceros. What provides the link-up between the message that comes into the brain and the reaction that occurs and shows itself in the horse's behaviour?

The answer is a combination of two elements: innate 'instinctive' tendencies and learning. The first the horse is born with intact and they are controlled by genes interacting with environment – they are species characteristic. The second is the product of the experiences of the individual animal's own lifetime.

Pre-determined behaviour follows programmes dictated by the patterns for living (see Chapter Two), the orientation that colours all the animal's activities, and which is moulded by millennia of an evolution process that has adjusted that animal to survive perfectly in its surroundings. Even animals that are reared in isolation develop behaviour patterns associated with these fundamental drives that are along normal lines. Eating and drinking, reproducing, avoiding and seeing off threats, preferring company – these are the contexts in which messages are assessed in the wild. Priorities are allocated depending on how usefully a stimulus fulfils these basic needs and the animal reacts accordingly. This ground-plan is present at birth, but from that point on it is never static. From the minute the foal arrives in the world, that plan begins to be influenced and moulded by experience. He starts to learn.

INSTINCT

What exactly are instincts?

Certain species-characteristic behaviour appears to have been pre-determined, programmed into an animal's genes by evolution. Such reactions appear to be rigid, not involving any choice or conscious decision and are not affected by experiences. Traditionally, these were labelled 'instinctive'. They satisfy some fundamental biological need and are stimulated by an external cue. So what sort of horse behaviour could be described as 'instinctive'? How many reactions are purely pre-set into his mental make-up and how many are actually tempered by learning? This is actually very difficult to figure out. Under the heading 'instinctive' behaviour, most people would list the foal's urge to find the teat and suckle, to stand and then move, the way a horse somehow seems to know he must run from danger, and later on, the drive to mate. But are those patterns so inflexible after all – and are they all inherent at birth? How many of them depend on the presence of the correct

trigger, and is this always external?

On further investigation, the boundaries between 'instinctive' and 'learned' behaviour are too blurred to make the customary definition a workable or meaningful one. For example, few behavioural patterns are absolutely rigid either in the way they are performed or under what circumstances. Horses are all different and will express a particular 'instinctive' action quite differently. A human threatening a horse for example, will cause a nervous animal to run, but might cause a frustrated or resentful horse to bite. Both reactions are fuelled by adrenalin, but many factors shape what response that rush of adrenalin provokes. Individuals might also express the same basic reaction differently each time it is carried out, modifying the behaviour according to the situation in which it is being used. What is more, many 'instinctive' behaviours need a great deal of practice to become effective. A foal knows he must struggle to his feet and put one foot in front of the other to move, but getting that movement efficient enough to contribute to his survival takes a lot of trial and error. Many patterns are only 'switched on' as an animal matures. The 'try walking' instruction is less urgent for a hunter than a hunted animal, and in humans is only activated at a certain age. From that start point again, it requires practice to perfect. Sexual behaviour is another obvious example of 'instinct' that has to wait for a cue, not external but internal – the body's production of sex hormones.

Equally hard to distinguish between are

> **'Horses are all different and will express a particular 'instinctive' action quite differently'**

reactions that appear to be inherent and those that are essentially 'learned' by copying other herd members, who are also all acting that way because 'everyone else is'. An animal is not necessarily born even with its fear of predators already intact. The herd reacts to predators fearfully almost by 'tradition' and so survives. The youngster learns, albeit very rapidly, and goes along with the crowd. In fact, no behaviour can be entirely free of environmental influences, which is why it is more useful to think in terms of 'strategies' rather than 'instincts'. As the distinction between inborn and learned behaviour soon becomes too vague to make sense, the term 'innate' is now preferred to describe any consistent reaction in a species that is 'released' by a cue or signal which the animal is able to recognise at birth, and so which must be pre-set into its genes.

SHEILA ROUGHTON'S VIEW

Sheila Roughton is a British Horse Society Instructor and Chief Examiner. Horses she has broken and trained to international level have been sold all over the world and have been selected for the German and Swiss showjumping teams and Italian Olympic eventing team. She has ridden internationally and in three-day events, and she has written several books on horsemastership, including Breaking and Training Your Horse.

' When you are training a horse, it is vital to always have your goalposts in the same place and only to move on to the next step when the previous one has been thoroughly understood. You must be logical and consistent and fair as far as you possibly can in everything that you do. There is no point thinking to yourself, "Oh the sun is shining today, it doesn't matter that you didn't quite go right into that corner,' and then the next day pounce on the horse when it does the exact same thing.

Fairness is terribly important in winning the horse's respect, and right from the beginning there must be respect from both sides – not only from the horse towards you, but from you towards the horse. That respect must never come through trying to dominate it. The horse must be working for you because he likes you, and the way a true friendship is made is when each party respects the other. Whether you are dealing with a young horse or an older one, the whole business of training is bluff to a degree. You only prevent the horse using his strength and size against you by never letting him know that he can, or giving him a reason to, and in that way everything is kept under control.

I believe that horses are more or less like children, you need to make a fuss of them when they are doing things right and tell them straightaway when they are not. But they should always be expected to do things in a certain, disciplined way, and in that respect you must treat them like adults. If a horse jumps a big fence for you or goes past something frightening, even though you should expect the horse to do it for you, still say 'Thank you very much' with a pat, because if he hadn't done it you would certainly be telling him off. It is also up to the trainer to avoid trouble before it occurs. For example, training should ideally always take place somewhere where the horse has the advantage of being able to do the exercise properly. Although there may be times when you are working in a situation that is not ideal, if ever I have an important major lesson to teach a horse, or if I hit a problem, I will always take him to an indoor

"When you are training a horse, it is vital to always have your goalposts in the same place and only move on to the next step when the previous one has been thoroughly understood." Sheila Roughton takes a young pupil back to basics over some ground poles.

school to work through. Be fair and be logical, so the horse has an idea if he is behaving along the right lines.

A horse will soon tell you when he is finding a request difficult or doesn't understand what he is being asked to do, and it is the rider's job to be aware of this. There are always going to be times when you need to ride through a difficulty, but never put the horse into a position where he is actually going to try and resist you, or where he gets worried and therefore tense.

Tension can come out in all kinds of ways,

whether it's simply the horse coming out of a shape or starting to pull, but generally it is due to the horse being over-faced in one way or another. If the horse becomes tense when you are trying to achieve something, there is no need to drop what you are doing completely, but, for example, you can come out of lateral work and do easy circles to relax him and get him going again before trying your shoulder-in once more.

Whenever you are introducing something new you must give yourself plenty of time and keep your aids very clear. There are certain moves, such as either asking for canter or asking for more bend around the leg, that are very similar, so the position and pressure of the leg must be very clear for the horse to know your meaning. It is small things like this which are good reasons why a novice rider should not be put with a novice horse, because it simply doesn't help the horse if he gets woolly aids. Every signal must be very clear, and when the horse reacts in the right way he must be rewarded through a stroke on the neck or a kind voice. Tension will creep in as soon as you try to do anything too difficult or for too long as he will start to get tired and to hurt, so you must stop as soon as the horse has done what you set out to achieve and he must always go into the stable in a relaxed, happy frame of mind. He must never go to bed worrying.

If there is a real problem in your training of any sort, the horse needs to be physically checked, and only when you can say there is nothing wrong should you consider he is being deliberately awkward. The horse's whole life must be a pleasant experience as far as possible. There are always ways to be nice to a horse without spoiling him, and I avoid the use of titbits.

A trainer needs endless patience and also a certain amount of experience to enjoy educating a horse, because he needs to understand the feedback he is getting. If a rider is not sufficiently educated they may never notice those little things which give you such a tremendous kick when they have gone right. I can trot a 20-metre circle and feel like I have just ridden around the Grand National if the horse has been working through in the right shape and without any resistance. However, if I asked an inexperienced rider to trot a circle they would probably be thinking: 'Is this all we're going to do today?' Even though they might be getting just the same feeling from the horse, they were not aware of it.

Feel is a gift to a certain extent, but there are ways an instructor can improve feel. It is important the rider is relaxed, as if you are not relaxed you certainly cannot feel – that applies to both the horse and the rider. Until the rider has feel and awareness they will never be able to think a training situation through for themselves. You cannot be on remote control when you are training a horse, you must be completely involved. The trainer must also have courage too and never be fainthearted in any way, as the horse will soon know. The mind potentially can have a very strong, positive influence. Riders must never forget that we are trying to create a partnership with another living animal like ourselves.

Matching the rider to the horse is absolutely vital, and it is where so many of us go wrong. You would not marry someone unless you were on the same wavelength. When you are training a horse it is a kind of marriage – a marriage of personalities. Physically and mentally, a rider needs to be able to understand and enjoy the horse he is riding – and to find the right horse for the job that is required. *'*

TYPES OF LEARNING

If an animal relied solely on innate and reflex responses it would not survive for long. A youngster has to learn – responses must be modified by exposure to experience. The example of the newborn's innate urge to find the teat, which then gives satisfaction, so the action is repeated until it is perfected, illustrates one very simple type of learning – by trial and error. The result of an action gives pleasure, so it is repeated. An action that fails to give pleasure, or produces discomfort, is less likely to be repeated. There is more than one type of learning, however, and most learning processes are much more involved than this. Learning is characterised by flexibility. What is learned may vary between individuals, and their resulting behaviour can alter too. There is much overlapping, but learning can be classified into five basic categories: habituation, associative learning, latent or exploratory learning, imprinting, and insight or problem solving.

HABITUATION

Adaptability, as we have seen, is a crucial ingredient in the survival recipe. If a behavioural reaction, however automatic, could never be reassessed or modified whatever the change in circumstances, the animal would soon make an error that might prove fatal. Sometimes situations which once posed no danger suddenly become life-threatening, or others which once represented a significant risk, necessitating constant alertness, simply no longer exist. In the second instance, life would become intolerable if the animal remained in a state of continual hyper-tension awaiting action that is unlikely ever to be needed.

The horse that allows us to walk behind him, feel him all over, pick out his feet and get on his back has become habituated to these actions because he has learnt, if his training and treatment has been correct, that they pose no threat. Habituation occurs when the animal gradually ceases to respond to repeated stimulation. If the stimuli prove not to be harmful, the animal learns to over-ride his natural response. Most horses learn to ignore noisy vehicles coming up from behind and passing within inches of their bodies. If put in this situation with no previous experience, the reaction would be dramatic and defensive – flight without thought. A gradual introduction, and the experience of many cars having passed without causing harm, habituates the horse to the traffic. Basically, he gets used to it and so does not respond to the cue to flee.

Many natural responses become diluted in this way – and it is just as well this adaptation takes place, because, without it, horses would be far less trainable. Behaviour adaptation is an on-going process in all animals' lives and it can happen remarkably quickly. It can also be undone quickly too – it is essentially only a temporary form of learning. The minute you think it is safe to believe a fear has been overcome, the learning can be 'forgotten' and original more primitive behaviour patterns can re-surface if the horse is put under stress, or if there is the tiniest change in the situation as a whole. The horse that is generally reliable in motor traffic could easily be panicked by the whir of a bicycle. A horse that is quite used to the road signs along his hacking route may be extremely alarmed by the sudden appearance of a new sign. The youngster who has learnt to accept being led and trotted up calmly at home could refuse to co-operate at all when faced with the same request at his first show.

Horses are not good at generalising

'An exercise tackled in several short sessions will be better absorbed'

experience, so this type of learning only becomes fully fixed when it has been habituated in as many different testing situations as possible. A young jumping horse that is understandably afraid of ditches (a natural response) needs to be schooled not only over open ditches, but tiger traps, trakehners and every form of obstacle involving an opening in the ground that the rider can find. Habituation does become more permanent the more often the 'new' situation is repeated, but the effectiveness depends, as always, on how thoroughly the learning was logged and the timing of the lessons. The original, innate response will become less and less dramatic until a cue is totally ignored – but if the cue is withdrawn for a while before being repeated the original response will return, albeit usually with less intensity than before and will then wane more quickly than the previous session. Research suggests that habituation is most thorough if it is effected by repeated short exposures to a cue rather than one long exposure. Hence, an exercise tackled in several short lessons will be better absorbed than if you hammer away on the same theme for too long in a single session.

ASSOCIATIVE LEARNING

There are two kinds of associative learning: 'classical conditioning', or 'Pavlovian' learning, and 'instrumental', 'operant' or 'trial and error' learning.

CLASSICAL CONDITIONING: This was first documented by the Russian physiologist Ivan Pavlov with his famous dogs. If a bell was always sounded immediately before food was produced, the dogs started salivating in anticipation of food at the sound of the bell alone, even when there was no food in sight. The sound had become connected with the food – the salivating reflex had become conditioned to the bell cue because they appeared so closely together in the past. Thus a cue that was previously unconditioned, becomes a conditioned stimulus, associated with a normal response with which it was not previously linked, and so will in future prompt that behaviour (now a conditioned reflex).

Like habituation, conditioning is an integral part of everyday existence for all of us. Associations form the basis of the majority of human and animal behaviour, including our likes and dislikes, habits, worries and motivations. In the wild, horses learn to associate certain unpalatable plants with certain colourations or shapes and so avoid eating them. They recognise the sound of a lion, and run to avoid being eaten. In general terms, conditioning allows animals to modify their behaviour so that maximum rewards are obtained and unpleasant experiences are avoided. Conditioning is based on reinforcement. The animal must associate a cue with a reward, lack of reward or a punishment. The animal remembers its past experiences and modifies its behaviour accordingly, usually at a sub-conscious level.

Associative learning like this cannot take place if the cue signal is given after the response, as no connection will be made between the two. It must come immediately before or else simultaneously. Repetition helps 'fix' the conditioning, as with other types of learning, and so does reward. If the rider clicks his tongue just as he feels the young horse about to strike off in canter, and he repeats this every time the horse goes into canter, the horse will soon begin to associate the click with the canter transition

Horses are excellent discriminators of detail, but very poor generalisers. Only a lengthy, involved training process, including tackling many different types of obstacle, will produce an event horse that can leap with confidence over anything he meets.

and produce the transition at the click signal. If the rider says 'Whoa' each time the horse is halted, the word comes to mean 'Stop forward movement' to the horse. Later, whenever the word is used it should slow, or stop the horse. Certain behavioural theories suggest that once an association has been formed between a stimulus or set of stimuli and an action, then it is likely with repetition that those stimuli will produce that reaction. In other words, it becomes a habit that gets stronger and stronger and harder to change – whether it is good or bad.

INSTRUMENTAL CONDITIONING: This is the basic trial-and-error type of learning. A hungry cat wanders about a room and finally jumps on to a chair. It is rewarded immediately with food. Rapidly it learns that jumping on the chair means food and so the cat immediately leaps up on the chair as soon as it enters the room. It has learnt to associate the reward not with a particular stimulus (as in Pavlovian conditioning) but with its own behaviour, discovered by chance. Instrumental conditioning is widespread among all life forms from

The 'shaping' of sets of conditioned responses allows extremely complex movements to be built up by the highly-trained horse.

humans to earthworms. It was first researched using experiments such as cages with levers to illustrate how rats and birds learned that pressing a lever brought food – reward. Then the reward would only be forthcoming when an extra signal was introduced, such as a light coming on – so the animal learned that light + lever = food. The animal could learn to react to avoid punishment also. If light + lever = no electric shock, then again, trial and error showed the animal the best way to react.

All experiments that test this type of learning involve presenting the animal with a choice: if it makes the 'right' choice it is rewarded, and the 'wrong' choice is punished, either directly or by the lack of reward. New responses are learnt to cues according to the reward, lack of reward or punishment that follows that specific cue. A very accurate response can be slowly and precisely built up using instrumental conditioning, a process that is termed 'shaping'.

At first the slightest correct reaction is rewarded. Once that is done well, only a further effort gets the reward. Later, to achieve the desired reward, the response may have to be quite complex and specific. An example would be teaching a young horse a lateral movement. At first he finds the task quite difficult, and so the reward of a pat or the cessation of aids after one step sideways is sufficient to encourage him to repeat that action when asked. When that is established, continuing to reward that single step would become less significant to the horse. The rider asks for several steps before the horse gets the indication he has done well. Progressively, the lesson is built up until the horse is rewarded only when the whole movement has been completed without any error – it is then 'shaped'.

Scientists attempting to assess an animal's ability to learn by trial and error look at the speed it takes to stop making errors, the length of time it can remember the 'lesson' without repeated re-runs, and the complexity of the 'lesson' to which it will respond. Conditioning, of one kind or another, provides the structure of most training. A horse's natural reaction to move away from the whip, for example, is sometimes used to initiate teaching of the leg aids. At the touch of the whip he moves forwards. The rider then uses his legs at the same moment as the whip. The horse comes to associate whip and legs. When this link is fixed, the use of the legs alone is enough to make the horse move forwards voluntarily – so long as their action ceases (so the horse is rewarded) once the forward movement is given. Once this basic conditioned response is established by such reinforcement, it can then be built on, using exactly the same principle, to make it more and more complex. Different leg positions mean different commands, and so on – so 'shaping' the horse's response. Rein aids are

developed in much the same way, and the two can then be combined to create increasingly subtle reactions. Much advanced training is based on the complex pairing of unconditioned and conditioned stimuli in this way.

LATENT OR EXPLORATORY LEARNING

This is not dependent on either rewards or constant repetition. It is the ability of the memory to store an experience unconsciously, without having an immediate or pressing need to do so. Horses are especially good at this and their capacity for recalling places, routes and locations is one example of latent learning in operation. This technique was tested using rats in mazes. They discovered that a hungry rat could find his way through a maze to food more quickly if he had already spent some time in the maze, with no reward or stimulus, beforehand. It was as though during its previous experience it had assimilated information that it later found it could put to use. This kind of exploratory learning is vital to wild animals, who use it to find their way easily around their territory.

IMPRINTING

This is the name given to a permanent, non-intentional type of learning that is not at all dependent on the repetition of associations. During imprinting, an early perceptual experience is indelibly marked into the animal's brain. It becomes, quite literally, a lasting impression. The clearest examples of imprinting have been studied in birds and animals of species that are particularly exposed or vulnerable when born and so their offspring need to learn very quickly. Nature seems to programme newborns to identify their parents – their protectors –

Imprint learning aims to exploit the newborn foal's drive to establish its identity and relationship to those around it, and it can be a powerful training tool.

very rapidly. These are the ones that the youngster needs to copy, learn from, and who he can expect to trust to take care of him. From this parent the creature learns its own identity. The sparrow knows it must be a sparrow, the magpie thinks 'magpie', and the foal 'horse'. This is all good news if the early experience was a normal one – but not so fortunate if the foal then thinks it is another species such as a human, and tries to indulge in in-built equine behaviour patterns with other humans! Imprinting does seem to occur beyond this first parental encounter to a degree, and it is increasingly thought to play a role in determining the youngster's behaviour later on in life. It is believed that many early experiences have some 'imprinting' effect. For example, a foal born into a feral herd that must learn from day one to run over rough terrain and be alert to dangers will always be more adaptable and resourceful than a domesticated foal who has his every need catered for.

Another aspect of the imprinting process is an indication that there are optimum times in the animal's life for certain experiences to be best absorbed so as to make their most powerful impression. It appears that once the 'deadline' is past the opportunity to learn in this particularly permanent and potent way is lost. A young horse who is deprived of equine company during its early years will lose the chance to have been 'imprinted' with normal equine social behaviour codes. If it has only been associating with humans for this time, it will regard itself as the same as us – and us as like himself – and is liable to treat us accordingly, as can be seen in some awkward, over-familiar hand-reared foals.

Imprinting has recently been latched on to as a training tool. Supporters believe that if the foundations are laid early enough for all that a youngster is going to need throughout life, then that baby has a head-start in his relationship with the human race. He will always be an obedient and amenable person who accepts humans and all they do without questioning or trauma. Imprint trainers in the United States start working with the foal within an hour of the birth. The aim is to desensitise it to potentially alarming sensations, sights and sounds and set up a bond of trust with humans – and a feeling of dependency. The foal might be rubbed over with plastic bags, for example, and held closely while still lying down so that it 'learns' that it must be submissive to a human because it is denied its innate flight option. The idea is that the foal bonds with both the mare and the human, as the man also stands above the foal rubbing and stroking it alongside the mare as she licks it. Many people would consider this an unacceptable intrusion that cannot help but interfere with normal mare-foal bonding. Advocates counter that the trainer never stands between mother and baby, only

alongside. During further sessions, all within the first day, the trainer will pick up feet, feel all over the areas where a saddle and girth will eventually go, and get the foal to lead and step forwards and backwards in response to pressure. Training then continues as the youngster is exposed to all the everyday activities it could expect to encounter in its life as a riding horse. Imprint training pioneer Dr Robert Miller even devises obstacle courses for foals to tackle with their handlers – all within a few weeks of birth.

INSIGHT AND PROBLEM-SOLVING

Insight learning is the forte of human beings, but not one of the horse's strong points, which is perhaps another reason why, from our perspective, we often perceive horses as being rather dull-witted. Insight learning can be defined as the immediate understanding of, and response to, a new situation without the need for trial and error. This would assume some process of reasoning, or intelligence.

Equines are simply not prone to flashes of inspiration. Perhaps this is because throughout evolution the kind of difficulties they encountered were not generally the sort that were most effectively solved by coming up with different ideas about potential solutions. The wild horse does not actually have much call for creative thinking or reasoning power. His natural reactions cater for every need, and few situations call for possibilities to be analysed and different methods attempted in order to discover a way around a difficulty. He has no need to think through cause and effect – his priority is to act first and reflect later.

So, if a horse is separated from his friends by a fence, he will gallop about madly

ABOVE: Horses learnt long ago to be balanced and athletic and to move effectively. We should not expect to improve on that – though we must be aware of how easily it can be destroyed.

BELOW: Resistance and tension are the only ways a horse has of saying "Hold on!" We should be looking at why a horse is resisting.

without realising that there is an open gate at one end of the field connecting the two pastures. In the end he will probably find the gap, but it is much more likely to be by accident as he careers around, rather than by calming down, considering the possibility and going to search for it. Perhaps if horses were less prey to their emotions, and had more capacity for insight, they would not be so vulnerable to situations of stress where they are torn between conflicting impulses, or when they are put into abnormal surroundings.

Insight is extremely difficult to assess even in human beings, as it is so hard to tell how spontaneous a 'brainwave' is, and how much it was actually based on previous experiences, trial and error, and all the other types of learning we have mentioned. However, if horses had no power of reasoning whatsoever it is highly unlikely they would have become the supreme survivors that they are. There are plenty of examples in horse behaviour of the use of logic and the application of past experience in one situation to help with a problem in a new context.

What is needed is for the environment to be right and the animal to be allowed to think things out for himself, or encouraged to put two and two together. Crucially, the horse must be in the right frame of mind – that is, calm and unpressurised – and the problem must be one that he is motivated to solve.

THE BALANCE TEAM'S VIEW

If there was one word that might sum up what drove Maureen Bartlett, Lesley Ann Taylor and Carol Brett to form the Balance Team, it would be "tension" – the tension that they saw in horses at all levels, often struggling to perform, hindered by

uncomfortable equipment and unsympathetic riding techniques that took little account of the horse's own natural way of going. Yet these were horses all too readily labelled 'awkward' or 'ungenerous' if they indicated their discomfort by some display of resistance. It was time to put the horse's needs first and to inject some feeling back into into our relationship with horses. Balance was founded to create a network of experts in the many fields related to equine care and education who are prepared to work together for the good of the horse.

MAUREEN BARTLETT:

‘ Going back through the history of riding, horsemanship is like most other things – you have trends. It seems to me that we have been going through a tremendous trend towards force in our dealings with horses. We are always trying to push the horse to adapt to our requirements, and what is convenient to us, rather than looking at his needs and respecting him as an independent creature who is incredibly honest and generous with us.

So many people feel they have to work hard at their riding. If only they would realise the sensitivity of the horse's mind, how quickly he picks things up and how much more finely-tuned his senses are than ours. No aid need ever be clumsy or strong. The problem lies in breaking down the arrogance of us human beings, imposing ourselves on them.

The main idea that we are trying to put across is that riding is 'wholistic'. Everything connects, you cannot look at one factor in isolation. You must look at all aspects, and, above all, never become blinkered. ’

LEFT: The Balance team (left to right): Carol Brett, Lesley Ann Taylor and Maureen Bartlett.

BELOW: Carol Brett measuring a horse for a correct saddle fitting. "To get the best from our horses we must look at ways of inhibiting them as little as possible."

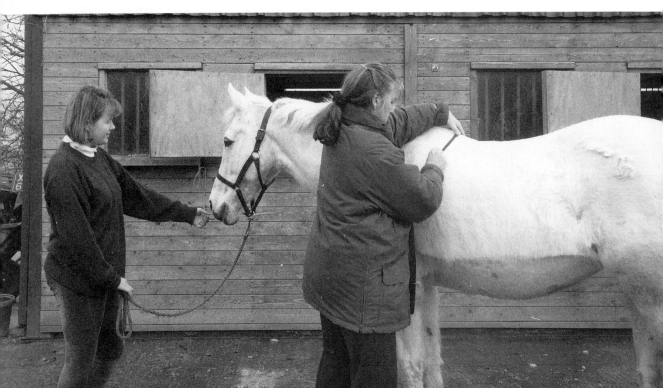

LESLEY ANN TAYLOR:

'Most people go into horses because they love them, and then somehow get led along the path that says that if they want to get anywhere they have to lose that feeling for the animal itself. Not everyone wants pressure on them to compete. You should be able to feel you can just enjoy your horse's company.

"Our prime objective at Balance is to take care of the horse first. Humans ride purely for leisure these days, so we believe we should pay for that pleasure and the price ought to be making the horse's welfare our priority. Much of our approach is about shifting the psychology of the person involved with the horse, learning to communicate with it at its own level, finding out what is acceptable to it and not asking more than it can cope with. What we must all learn to respect is that the horse is, in its own way, a very well-developed creature that has been evolving for far longer than mankind. Horses learnt long ago how to be balanced and athletic and move efficiently and we shouldn't expect to be able to improve on that – though we must be aware of how easily it can be destroyed.

The horse itself is our best guide to its own needs. In a true partnership between a horse and rider it is accepted that the horse is entitled to an 'opinion' and that, rather than simply telling the horse what to do, we should have the humility to listen to it and respect its sensitivity. The key to this much more rewarding approach is that the rider must be totally focused with the horse – and in the moment with their horse – rather than thinking only about the position of their hands or legs or which direction they are travelling. The horse is our most valuable teacher. A lot of good riding is simply listening - it is about dynamic communication with your horse. Riders must relax and start feeling what is underneath them.

We like to get our riders riding bareback as it gives them a wonderful appreciation of that link they have with their horse. As a trainer you can watch the shifts going on and see how tiny, subtle changes in the riders' bodies are affecting the horse. It also gives the riders a sense of the responsibility they bear for their own part of the bargain. In my mind, riders who get on the horse in a bad mood or when they are tired and don't really want to ride, shouldn't ride. A rider should either get on and pay attention to their horse and work with it as a partner, or not get on in the first place.

From our own experience fitting saddles, we have found that it is possible to be very kind to a horse on the ground but, unwittingly, very cruel to it on its back and from a psychological point of view. Many times we come across owners with strong emotional links with their horses, which then cannot understand why every time that person gets on their back it hurts. From the horse's point of view, having this contrary experience day after day is quite damaging. We try to persuade people to put aside at least a month as a remedial period, working the horse without a saddle so it has no restrictions at all and can rediscover how to

'Riders who get on the horse in a bad mood or when they are tired, shouldn't ride'

move and let all the psychological blocks go – and give the rider a chance to let go also.

Many horses are confused and demoralised because they are often dealing with a situation where they are living in an unnatural environment, virtually isolated, not allowed to socialise naturally with their own kind and fed an unnatural diet. Then they may have a saddle put on that causes discomfort, and on top of that climbs a rider who gives the horse inconsistent information most of the time.

Our message is that we make the most progress by staying within the horse's comfort zone at all times. That comfort zone includes the physical, the psychological and the emotional. We must stay within those boundaries – yet all too many trainers do the exact opposite. Every rider must learn to take responsibility for the welfare of their own horse and, when necessary, dare to question their trainer if they are not happy. It is time for a tremendous shift in emphasis towards respect for the horse. **'**

CAROL BRETT:

' The more aware we can become of how our own bodies work and the connections in our bodies, the more understanding we can have of the basic things a horse can do. When the two movements, the rider and the horse, are blended together rather than one imposing on the other, that is when you get the most beautiful work. For example, I often wonder what heights the horse would be capable of jumping if its rider were truly out of its way and it was able to use its body – considering the fences they still manage to clear with all the restrictions that most of them jump

with. The hardest thing is for the riders to learn to let go. One of the first exercises I do with most riders is to make them aware of what speed their horse can work at most efficiently – and by this I mean speed in miles per hour, which you rarely hear horse people talk about. Once a horse slots into that speed he picks up his own natural rhythm and will start to let go all the tensions in his body.

I ask people to tell me what speed their horse's trot is and say to them, it doesn't matter whether the number you say is right or wrong. What matters is what that trot feels like to them and what speed the horse feels best at. Then, if they have said say 7mph, I ask them to try what they would call a 6mph or 8mph trot and see what that feels like. Once they have that feeling, they don't need me any more, they can go for a ride on their own tomorrow and know exactly what their horse's optimum trot is like.

A horse will respond to any shift we make in our bodies with total honesty, so what we get as riders is a mirror of ourselves constantly thrown back at us. Many riders are not comfortable with that, particularly in the highly competitive world where too often people are looking for a robot to ride. When the rider is so blocked, the horse is blocked.

This 'harsh' attitude has escalated since the trend for competition because everyone has this feeling that they must try and ride their horses 'on the bit'. However, for a variety of reasons many horses cannot go on the bit, often because their saddle is bad for them and stimulates the reflexes that make a horse hollow its back, so the hind legs cannot engage, no matter how hard the horse is trying. Resistance and tension are the only ways a horse has of saying to us:

'Hold on!' What we should be looking at is why a horse is resisting, and not just saying 'Every horse resists', or 'It's a chestnut mare, what do you expect?' Our saddle-fitting work developed from our training methods.

The horse is designed perfectly both physically and mentally to be a horse. We cannot improve on nature, and as soon as we start putting any equipment on a horse, the only potential we have is to inhibit. None of the training aids or tack used by riders can make the horse move any better than it can in nature, because the horse is designed to move free. So, to get the best from our horses we must look at ways of inhibiting them as little as possible. That is how the Balance saddles developed, because we found with so many horses that as soon as their saddle was put on, immediately their movement became restricted, even before the rider got on board. People can develop a whole riding career working with a horse that cannot move its body correctly, and yet expect that horse to collect and engage – and they put any resistance down to 'bad character'! **'**

5 HOW INTELLIGENT ARE HORSES?

There is a school of thought that argues that horses cannot be very bright, because if they were, they would be unlikely to let man anywhere near them, let alone on their backs, forcing them to do all kinds of unnatural and extremely risky activities. The horse's remarkable willingness to please certainly has led him into all kinds of deep waters – but this cannot be held up as an example of lack of intelligence, because it is perfectly explicable in terms of his natural social behaviour. The horse is a herd animal who lives to socialise and responds to firm directives and set rules of play. There is nothing particularly astonishing about the way a horse so easily confers his loyalty upon a two-legged friend and leader, and accepts the regulations we impose. Every member of any community becomes conditioned to live by certain social rules and is not considered unintelligent for it.

In fact, the horse's adaptability and trainability point more to great intelligence. After all, he is undoubtedly far more accomplished at learning our language than we are his. We expect him to exist and perform in a largely alien environment. To get along as a stranger in a strange land, he not only has to work out what we want of him, but then learn how to do it too. Now that is problem-solving! It is likely that intelligence involves far more than insight learning alone. More probably it encapsulates all the different types of learning, some of which horses are extremely good at.

DAVID BROOME'S VIEW

David Broome, showjumper of world renown, has competed at the very peak of his sport for almost forty years. His tally of international honours includes two Olympic bronze medals, three European Championships, the 1970 World Championship, six National Championships, and five King George V Gold Cups. On his retirement from international teams in 1994, he had notched up a record of 106 Nations Cup appearances, a third of them winning ones. Today he concentrates on training novices and young riders, and on his work as Chairman of the BSJA. In 1995 he was awarded the Companion of the British Empire (CBE) for services to showjumping.

‘ Looking back at some of my greatest horses, the characteristic they all held in common was a genuine desire to please and do their best. If they had not had that, they would have fallen by the wayside. When a horse goes in that ring he needs to want to achieve; without that you

"The key to a great partnership is in the horse's training. If the horse is prepared well, then he is equipped to face the challenge, is comfortable in his job and has trust in his rider." David Broome competing at Hickstead.

are in trouble from the start. You also need a horse with ability. The good horses certainly know the big occasion and they rise to it. They are cocky devils and they know they are good. I remember once in a parade at a big show in Lancashire I was there with Sportsman as the centrepiece, along with Red Rum. These two horses just stood there and eyed each other up – neither was going to give way to the other. It was a case of: 'Who the hell does he think he is? I'm the king around here!' It was lovely to watch.

I would say that showjumping is less demanding mentally on a horse than dressage, but the showjumper has to have more talent in one particular direction than the event horse. Showjumping horses do need to be brave, but they must also have their eye on the ball. It's funny, you can get horses that will jump a fence three times and then spook at it when you walk in to get their prize – Mr Softee was one of those. And you might get quite a good pole jumper who dislikes water jumps – they are all different. Usually a horse with a fair amount of talent is brave. And yet the ones who jump the big wall in the Puissance, are often slightly 'kinky' and not particularly good over a normal course. There are always exceptions, but as a rule those ones have plenty of ability, plenty of scope, but are, perhaps, short on brain power!

A horse with a nap in him has always got a negative wave running through his brain. He's never trying to please you because he's always thinking of how he can 'do' you. When you are talking about placing a priority on cleverness or obedience in a jumping horse, a lot comes down to the breeding of the horse. With the German warmblood horse, you always have to open the work manual at page one and progress through it. He's probably been factory-bred, never been given any initiative and he's fine so long as there is a button there for everything you want him to do. In comparison, the Irish-bred horse has been born out in the field, he's survived the chain harrow and the 40-gallon drum and the barbed wire that's everywhere – he's done all that for three or four years and had to look after himself, so it's in him.

The different types of horses somehow reflect the characters of their owners – the German, the English and Irish, and then you've got the American-bred, who's a different beast again. I think we all ride them the way we do because that's the best way to ride them. The Germans tend to dominate their horses because they have to. The Irish horse has a lot of survival sense in him, so he will look after himself. Good riders will soon adapt to get the best out of any horse, but the breeding in Europe has improved so much now that the warmbloods

> *'I always like to talk to my horses because they do understand your tone of voice'*

are dominating the sport today. Personally, I would rather have the horse with a bit of intelligence and self-reliance about him than the slow-witted one you have got to push.

The best horses cannot just be doing as they are told. I think that if a horse is only doing what he's told, he doesn't care too much. Good horses must enjoy their work, otherwise they couldn't do it – and they wouldn't try as hard. Good horses cover up your mistakes and bad ones will expose them. But basically, if he's a careful horse he will want to jump it as much as the rider does. A good horse will help you out an awful lot. I'm a great believer in the fact that the better trained a horse is, the more obedient he is, the happier he is. The key to that great partnership lies in the horse's training. If the horse is prepared well, then he is equipped to face the challenge, comfortable with his job and has trust in his rider.

Communication is the factor on which everything depends. The horse must be as soft as you can get him. Every 'hinge' in his body must be able to respond. There must be no 'no-go' areas where, if you ask him to do something, he refuses to do it. He must be fully obedient so that all the aids are available to him and to you – for you to be able to use them and for him to be able to understand them.

After all, everything you teach the horse, he can do on his own quite naturally. Our game is communication. We have to communicate what we want. What might work for one rider and one horse might not work for another. That's the old partnership game – the understanding. Two living things thinking like one. You have to fit around the mental outlook of the horse. Old Sunsalve, he used to love going with a bit of flair and dash, and, luckily, as I was 20 when I had him, I could go along with him, but I couldn't do it now! Philco was always the arrogant fellow – we used to call him the 'Arrogant Yank', he was always so cocky but so big-hearted. You used to have to get him to compromise his enthusiasm to get him to do what you wanted him to, because he had all the ability but you had to get through to him that he just couldn't do it at 90 miles an hour, which, being an ex-racehorse, he thought he could. He had to come back and listen to you. But as the years went by he got more of his own way, I'm afraid!

Sportsman used to walk in the ring and have a look around the course himself, he was that intelligent. Mr Softee always tried to please you, but Manhattan, he had all the scope and ability in the world, but getting him to concentrate and not make a stupid mistake was almost impossible. Of the more recent horses, Countryman was a lovely horse, but you did not dare to make a move on him because somehow he would tense up. Lannegan got so excited. He used to be laid-back and I could always go against the clock on him, but one day he just cottoned on and was never quite the same again after that. I could have done with him staying a bit cooler in his brain but he always got ambitious – especially after about fence six or seven when he got keener and keener.

Wildfire, my very first good horse, he used to stop before I had him. I remember it now, riding him out of the yard there into the field. I was 17 and it was October time and I just gave him three either side in quick succession and basically he never did it again. He was a funny lad because he would allow you one go to put his bridle on, and if you didn't get it over his ears in that time, you'd had it. He was quite happy to put his head down and let you have one try, but then no. He always looked vicious and bad-tempered and wound his old tail up, but he had great ability and always gave his best. I found him a lovely horse and we really hit it off.

I always like to talk to my horses because they do understand your tone of voice. I seem to be able to create a relationship with a horse quite well. That does not mean to say I could make one jump that cannot or will not, but most horses are fairly easy-going. They just want a happy life and they're fairly forgiving too, which is just as well.

I think you find a great partnership when both horse and rider think as one; when whenever you want to do something it becomes a lovely, easy action – like water over a waterfall, it just happens. When you are both thinking along the same lines there is a kind of telepathy, a sympathy between the horse and the rider. The rider makes the right moves and the horse is quick enough and obedient enough to do as beckoned. When everything is happening well, it's a lovely relationship you have going with a horse. You have got this beast below you which is about ten times heavier than you are, and with a touch of a finger he will do anything you want him to do. It's very

> **'When you are both thinking along the same lines there is a kind of telepathy between horse and rider'**

special. Most problems come from the rider not being able to exercise all of his options, and from not making the work pleasant enough for the horse. You have to have a situation where, hopefully the rider will know what to do and the horse will respond to his request. The rider's job is, by using the right pace and rhythm and getting him into the right shape, to put him on the right spot at the right time so the horse can then jump the fence – so the horse can do the jumping. The less obedient the horse is, the more difficult it is to ride to that right spot and the greater the chances are that you won't arrive at it. Then life gets difficult for the horse and he gets upset, which makes life even more difficult because he gets more and more anxious. The whole thing is a slippery slope. Hence, the nicer he's trained the easier it is to ride him to the fence correctly and so the happier the horse is.

The challenge is knowing your horse. In showjumping you do need nice horses with talent before you start, because you can't make a silk purse out of a sow's ear. What you can do, very easily, is ruin a silk purse – that doesn't take a lot of doing. The art is, when you have got something, to make it better.

You get some people who can get on with most horses – like Michael Whitaker, he can ride anything, but there are still some horses that go better for him than others. Unless a horse suits you, there's not a lot of point carrying on with it. If you're a soft rider you need a soft sort of horse. If you're strong, you can cope with a strong-willed horse better than some. A ham-fisted rider on a delicate animal will never go right, so it's important you are matched.

I think horses are wonderful, because no matter what's happened in your life you can get out there and you've got this completely fresh thing to start with – the horse and you. You can go out there in the woods, the world's crashing down all around you – and there's this horse underneath you who's trying to please you. You can relate to this animal. He will lift you, he will save your day for you. We are struggling to get into his mind and hopefully to communicate and to make his life better for him as well. You have got to get on well, the two of you together, and then you will improve each other's lot. **,**

WHAT IS INTELLIGENCE?

The difficulty in measuring intelligence comes in trying to compare like with like. The horse shies violently at a bird flying out of the hedgerow and it is hard to resist the temptation to call him 'stupid', especially when he took not the slightest bit of notice of a jet plane roaring overhead only a minute before. In equine terms his behaviour was totally logical – if something flutters in the peripheral vision, move! But attack is unlikely to come from directly overhead.

All living species have made it through to the present day because they are brilliant at being what they are – so long as they are within their own environment and judged by their own criteria and are not fishes out of water. Nature is teeming with examples of breathtaking, adaptive behaviour from creatures that have become geniuses at 'being themselves' and are constantly showing how clever they are in their own style. Each is dealing with its own problems, in the context of its own medium and that medium's demands. It is impossible for one species to make objective judgements on the wisdom, or otherwise, of another's actions because they cannot be compared. The hunter and the hunted, for example, have quite different outlooks on the world. A prey animal cannot afford to make a mistake. Its reactions therefore tend to be rapid and dramatic, often violent, and there is particular sensitivity to experiences associated with pain and fear which can give rise later on to some apparently odd behaviour when similar circumstances are encountered again. The nervousness and cautious nature of horses is never an indication of stupidity – it is an illustration of the intelligence of a prey animal. In contrast, if a predator should have a failure, all is not lost. He simply logs the experience and what it has taught him, then turns his attention to seeking out another potential meal. He needs to develop cunning, whereas a prey animal does not.

When it comes to problem-solving, how much of homo sapiens' legendary superiority is down to the simple fact that we have hands, when horses are stuck with hooves? Equines are simply not built to be constructive and creative. We are able to use insight learning much more effectively, because we can try a huge range of manipulative options when considering how to solve a particular dilemma. The horse has never required precise manipulative skills – what he does need is dealt with very effectively by his lips. As a result, when it comes to facing a situation that requires thinking around, he has relatively few practical options open to him. My Welsh Mountain pony is a positive Houdini who has worked out exactly where to stand in order to nip through the gate as another horse is led out giving you the least chance

of stopping him – in other words, he is trying to use the skill he does have, fast locomotion, to solve the problem of getting to the other side. Likewise, he will jump out of a stable if it is physically possible. But if he cannot use his legs, he will improvise and try manipulation as best he can– so he will undo virtually any lead-rope knot within minutes by persistent nibbling at it. Who can say that if he had fingers he would not be instantly unlocking the door or gate to let himself out, or untie his knot? He certainly recognises the problem: he would rather be somewhere else; knows the solution – 'I need to get through that gate/door, or I need to undo that knot'; but has not got the best physical means of implementing that solution. He does the best he can, and often succeeds!

STRENGTHS AND WEAKNESSES

So, a type of intelligence that is very well-developed in one species might not be so in another, which might have other strengths more appropriate to its own natural environment. If this is the case, what are horses good at?

With such well-developed retentive memories and their sensitivity to detailed stimuli, horses can be brilliant discriminators – if the objects or signals they are being asked to distinguish between are meaningful to them. Their survival depends on knowledge founded on noticing minute differences – in other horses, in terrain, in plants and so on. What is important to a horse is to be able to discriminate, and not

'The cautious nature of horses is an illustration of the intelligence of a prey animal'

In the wild, survival would depend on remembering fine details of the environment and subtle changes in it from season to season – where the water source lay, areas of tricky terrain, which plant tasted bitter and so might be dangerous. During the grazing process every leaf and stem is sifted and assessed.

to generalise, because generalising could be risky. Blindly reacting in the same way to similar situations without noting and analysing changes in detail might leave the horse open to danger and would, indeed, be rather stupid. The sensible horse takes every situation as it comes.

Many social creatures have superb discriminating skills. The herring gull needs to locate her own chick among a colony of thousands. A ewe can identify her own lamb's cry among dozens of bleating newborns. A horse who dislikes the artificial smell of medication in his feed, can pick out every pony nut and leave just a heap of granules at the bottom of the bucket, however well his owner thought it had been mixed in.

DISCRIMINATION

The horse's amazing ability for visual discrimination is illustrated in the famous story about Clever Hans, a horse who belonged to a German named von Osten. The man believed that he had proved horses as intelligent as men, because his horse could not only count, but could also do mathematical calculations and solve problems of logic. Hans would be asked a question, such as what is 3 x 4, and would give his answer by tapping his foot 12 times. Crowds were astonished by the horse's ability and he was set increasingly difficult problems, which he continued to answer correctly, even when Herr von Osten was replaced by another trainer to eradicate the possibility of fraud.

Eventually the secret of Clever Hans was exposed. When the horse could see his 'questioner', he always got his answers correct. When he was put behind a screen, he failed. With astounding skill at picking up nuances of body tension, Clever Hans had learnt to tap his foot until the trainer's body literally 'told' him he had reached the right number and should stop, when he would get his reward. The trainer's anticipation was matched by the audience, who also knew when the horse was approaching the correct answer. Between them all, they unconsciously revealed this to a herd animal acutely sensitised to body language and the way it reveals mood. Hans was motivated to use his discriminatory ability by the reward of pleasing his owner. Sadly, Herr von Osten was very disappointed in him when the truth was revealed, though in reality he should still have been amazed at how the horse had so ingeniously worked out a way of getting the reward he sought.

If a meaningful urge is there, horses can show their ability to discriminate and solve simple perceptual problems even in more formal 'laboratory' tests. One study discovered that horses learned to identify correctly one particular pair of shape patterns (for example, a square and a circle) out of up to 20 pairs of different combinations in order to get reward. In addition, the majority showed almost no memory loss whatsoever of the exercise and performed with almost equal accuracy when it was repeated a year later

What horses are not so good at is generalising – making assumptions about the relationships between objects, or

'In general, the horse's best and most effective solution to a problem is to run'

particularly, abstract concepts. If the horses in the above experiment were then asked to pick out the pattern that was 'different' in a line of two squares and one circle, this might be possible. Far harder would be a request to select a picture of a fish as being the 'odd one out' in a line that was, say, sparrow, fish, magpie. Faced with a line of number figures, the horse would have no clue that two were 'even' numbers and only one an 'odd' number because he has no concept at all of mathematics – so these are hardly fair questions! Where horses fail is in tests devised by humans for humans, or by humans for horses but from a human's viewpoint! Either the question has no meaning to a horse, or the horse has no drive to solve the puzzle, or it is not sufficiently equipped to do so. Often the puzzle does get solved, but in a way that appears random and haphazard and therefore seems to owe more to accident than purposeful thought.

A popular IQ test involved an animal being placed in a box with a bowl of food visible outside, which could be reached by pressing a lever. Monkeys impressed scientists by examining the lever and trying possibilities until they finally hit upon the solution. Dogs, by contrast, paced around the box, nose to the ground, until the lever was accidentally activated. This test, which appeared to show the monkeys to be far brighter, was hardly fair to the dog. A monkey's natural inclination is to scrutinise by manipulation and overcome obstacles such as when cracking a nut out of a shell. A dog travels to find his food. He may not be so good at insight learning, but trial and error still got him there in the end, against the odds. Many animals, including horses, tend to go about problem-solving in a similar way to the dog in the cage. Having decided what the problem is, or realised what is being asked of them, they will run through the various options they are orientated to, turning firstly to those that experience/memory tells them worked in that kind of situation before.

As we have already seen, horses appear to be poor at solving 'detour' problems, often galloping about in blind distress when separated from their friends, totally ignoring an open gate. But once again, their reaction is perfectly natural to them. In general, the horse's best and most effective solution to most problems is to run, so setting up a 'detour' type test to try and quantify his intelligence is stacking the odds against him. The instinct to run is so strong that the horse finds it extremely difficult to 'break out' of this mould of thinking and view the situation from a different perspective that then might yield more possible solutions. Instead he gets more and more frustrated that his natural solution does not seem to be working – and his emotions blinker his brain still further.

INDIVIDUAL TALENTS

What about comparing the intelligence of individuals within a species? The dictionary definition of intelligence is the 'capacity to apply old experiences to help tackle fresh challenges', and its level is assessed by the speed with which an individual can do this. Some horses are certainly quicker on the uptake than others, and in this they are no different from ourselves. Human society is made up of a fabric of individuals all with their own strengths and weaknesses. Individual horses are undoubtedly the same

– riding would certainly be dull if they were not. There are the emotional types who readily let their feelings blot out their intellect or excitement overcome their better judgement. Cold-blood breeds that tend to be more stolid, calmer characters can learn more quickly than the supposedly more intelligent, but rather over-emotional, hot-bloods, who frequently have to be introduced to new things slowly and reassured every step of the way. A problem is that the cool customers can equally easily become dull, bored and unmotivated if that intellect is never stretched. If he is given cause for resentment or anger, he tends to shut himself off completely, where the reactive Thoroughbred or Arab is more likely to respond by getting into a panic or becoming aggressive. Even within the broader confines of breeds and temperaments, some individuals learn fast, others more slowly. Some realise after only one knock that touching a jump pole is uncomfortable and therefore not a good idea if it can be avoided. Others can go on hitting them for six all their lives without a care in the world! Top-level jumping horses, of course, often have a lot of their thinking done for them. The rider might not necessarily want too independent a thinker underneath him. He educates the horse to go in physical balance and to 'do as he's told'. The horse must listen for the signal that says 'take off now' at the moment the rider judges is the optimum, whatever the horse's own 'opinion' on the subject. This is not a foolish horse, but a very obedient one who has learned his lessons well. He is, however, totally at the mercy of his rider's ability. His training has masked not only his own judgements but also his own natural inclination, which might have been to be bold or to be cautious, to be reactive or to be sluggish. Many competition riders might say

Every animal, humans and equines included, has to learn how to learn. Perfecting conditioned responses and linking them to create complicated reactions takes a great deal of practice.

species is that the animal has to 'learn how to learn'. Perfecting conditioned responses and linking them to create more complex reactions takes practice. As the animal gets more experienced at learning, it learns more and more quickly and is able to absorb increasing amounts of increasingly subtle conditioning. A foal is a real novice at the learning game, but he improves rapidly and is soon taking on board experiences at a fast rate. Just like a young child, this is the period when his ability to absorb learning is at its greatest. When a horse reaches an advanced level of dressage, for example, it could be considered in the equine 'mastermind' league.

Understanding the basic structure and mechanics of learning, being able to assess an individual horse's learning ability and capitalise on what he is good at, achieving the best from each horse he comes across – this is the job of the trainer.

KAREN O'CONNOR'S VIEW

Karen O'Connor is one of the USA's leading event riders and a regular member of the US Equestrian Team. Her career has encompassed success at many of the world's greatest three-day events, a tribute to a rider who is respected for her sympathetic style, tenacity and courage in overcoming setbacks. Karen trained under Olympic medallist Jimmy Wofford in the USA, and she has recently returned to Virginia after a four-year spell in England working with Mark Phillips. With her current top horse, Biko, she was third at Badminton 1995 and eighth at the 1995 European Open Championships.

they do not want a horse that is too intelligent, because the bright ones are most adept at finding ever more ingenious ways of avoiding doing activities they are not keen on. Evasion is relatively easy for even the smallest of ponies, so for a horse to do a job particularly well without resistance it seems to follow that he must be enjoying it.

What is known about intelligence in any

First impressions are vital when it comes to deciding whether a horse is going to make a good eventer. For me, there has to be a chemistry there. If, at first glance, I'm not taken by the horse, a hundred people couldn't talk me into loving that horse the way you need to be successful in this sport. Having said that, if you were to break the horse down into parts that are important, the eye to me is the most important part of the body. They have to have that 'look of eagles', that positive and intelligent look. To be a three-day event horse they need to be intelligent, so the eye, to me, must be strong – strong-willed – but also relaxed and confident. You can tell a lot about a horse's temperament from the look they give you.

I want a horse that has the look that says: 'What would you like me to do?' Not the look that says: 'I don't want to know.' Many times when you find a bad temperament, it is man-made or uncooperative because the horse has had a fright or bad experience. It takes a bit of knowledge to figure out whether that temperament is something the horse has been born with or whether it has been created. The temperament is everything, because you can have the most physically talented horse in the world, but if in his mind he is not relaxed and wanting to get the job done, you will always be fighting him.

I once had a horse that had a couple of bad falls before I got the ride, and he was very shaken up by them. When I first started riding him, he would come to a pole on the ground and stop and tremble. This was a horse that had already gone to middle-level eventing. He would hang in the back of his stable not talking to anyone, afraid of everything. If you take on that type of horse you need to be very experienced, and you

'When I first started riding him, he would come to a pole on the ground and stop and tremble'

have got to have the time and patience to give the horse what he needs. That became a very successful horse for me – very brave and very successful. But having said that, there were rules that we lived by. I would never ever ask him to do something I didn't have complete confidence that he could do. There was nothing left up to guess-work, because it would have betrayed all of the trust that we had built up. I trusted him 100 per cent and he trusted me 100 per cent.

We spent a lot of time in the box with that horse. With all of our horses we use techniques to 'dominate' them, but in a completely non-aggressive way. We get the horse to put his head down, so, when you touch the halter, the horse will put his head down to the ground and leave it there, and you can do whatever you want with him. When you have a horse that will put its head down, or go forwards, you have a horse that will do anything you want. For example, when a horse doesn't want to go into a van, how does he react? His head goes up. If he doesn't want his bridle on, he braces against you and flings up his head. In the wild, if he wants to run or to fight, it's all 'up' – that's how they dominate the situation. So, you teach a horse to be below you, so you are in a dominant position, but with the least amount of aggression. You do not pull his head down, but you can teach him how to put it down properly.

We have a round pen, and we use it to start off all the horses from the earliest ages. When you pull them up in the round pen they are completely free, no tack on or anything, and they turn to look at you. If you turn around at that point and walk away they will follow you. That's the relationship you have to have. The principles of working in a round pen basically are: if you give me that look, I will give you a rest; if you are away from me, or run around me, I will keep you running. So you get through to the horse by a rest-work situation. The horse learns to be completely trusting of you, as you are above him. When you ride him, you are above him all the time, so he has to have that kind of relationship with you.

If you are in a situation like I am, with many horses to ride, you have to have professional grooms taking care of the horses and you must teach the grooms to deal with them in the way you want. Because that person handles that horse on a day-to-day basis they have everything to do with that horse's success. We spend a lot of time and effort on the relationship between groom, rider and horse. When the groom is experienced you trust them 110 per cent with that horse.

Regardless of which discipline you are competing in, the basis of all success is relaxation and confidence, but that confidence can be acquired through correct training. Having said that, you would not want the same relaxation for the dressage as you would for cross-country, because for cross-country the horse has to have aggression, but a controlled aggression. In dressage you would not want an aggressive attitude in a horse, but you do have to have controlled power.

The horse has got miles more power than the person has, but you have to control and focus that power. So, for the different disciplines, it is the rider's responsibility to manage pressure. If you get into a competitive situation and the horse feels tense about the dressage for example, or the rider is worried about the showjumping or a particular fence, at that point it is about management of pressure – how you prepare yourself and how you portray it to the horse. The horse's temperament can be very affected by the rider's management of their own self. Temperament for dressage has to be relaxed and it has to be powerful, very much a concentration and focus between the horse and rider – in terms of technique, the horse basically being between the rider's leg and hand. In the jumping phases it is also about the horse's self-carriage and balance, but now the power has to be contained between the rider's leg and the jump.

If I asked you to touch your toes with your palms on the ground now, you probably could not do it, but if I asked you every day for three weeks, you probably could. That is the rider's job: to take a horse who only wants to move his leg that far, and make it go that far. Then, the horse has more co-ordination and more strength. Then it becomes easy for him because he has more confidence in his work. That is the basis of training – plus keeping it fun for the horse.

Always try to put the horse into a situation where he's enjoying himself. If the horse is not going to reach the highest levels, the rider or trainer must come clean with their own instincts and say: 'Okay, I'm not going to carry on here, I'm going to put

'Always try to put the horse into a situation where he is enjoying himself'

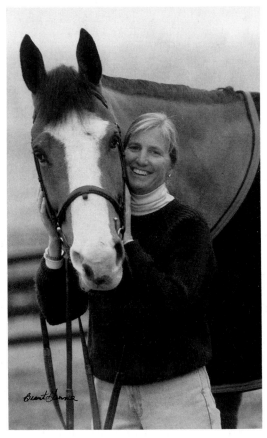

Karen O'Connor with Biko – "a great friend and a fun, fun, horse to work with because he's so intelligent."

Photo: Brant Gamma.

this horse into a situation which is better for him.' Maybe it should be doing dressage or go to a young rider, or go hunting. The horse is not a vehicle for the rider's success and should never be allowed to be treated as such. But it can take time for a rider to come to terms with this.

It also takes time to bring out the potential in a horse. Biko, currently one of most successful horses, is a real clown. He

has a very personable personality. He will eat anything from a Polo mint to a ham sandwich and do tricks for you to get food – he's everybody's pet. But when we bought him as a five-year-old he had only just been backed and, being so big and backed so late, and with his temperament being so 'big' too, he was a bit afraid of things. For two years it took three people just to get me on him. We spent months doing everything we could possibly think of with the horse so he would become comfortable with himself – going out into the countryside, jumping into creeks, trotting back and forward over a bale of hay in the field – little things, but so important, because this horse had the talent to really shine but was so insecure within himself. It was a question of getting the education to break into his potential. We didn't compete him for two years. There was no point competing him as a young horse and asking him to stay in control when he wasn't capable of it – that's what the management of pressure is about.

Biko is a great friend and a fun, fun horse to work with because he's so intelligent. I have had to figure out how to ride him because he is 17.3hh and I am not really big enough for him, so it has taken many years to learn and bring him to a level where we could communicate, especially in terms of balancing him across country.

He chooses his friends very carefully and will not be handled by just anybody. Again, that's why the groom is so important. Biko has only ever had three people work with him in his life, and all have loved working with him – that's made all the difference. If you try to make him do something, or get sharp around him, he will get real angry and withdraw into himself, become introverted and close doors so he can't hear you.

With horses of Biko's intelligence, there's a

Competing at Badminton 1995. "Whatever the discipline the horse is intended for, the trainer has two essential tasks. The first is to develop a line of communication with the horse... The second is to create a better athlete." **Photo: Trevor Meeks, Horse & Hound.**

fine line whether they are too intelligent to be ridden. If you get one that is so smart, so precocious and independent, they are like artists – they are difficult, they are articulate in what they do, so they are difficult to manage. For that quality of horse you have to be pretty on the ball. They have personalities, they are cheeky, aggressive at times, they sulk, they are too courageous sometimes , and then they will do something really stupid like shy at something and, being so athletic, when they shy they almost get you off. There are times when you

wonder how a horse that can be so afraid of a leaf on the ground will go and jump into the lake at Badminton! But that's a real trait of a top event horse – they can be really spooky, because they see a lot, and when you can channel that energy into one job, they really light up.

We want our horses to blossom out – that is very important – so we really try to develop the personality of each horse. Prince Panache is a very insecure horse, but he is also very sensitive and very smart. So the pair of them, Biko and Nache, have a great

115

friendship, almost as if they are married! They go around a lot together. Out in the field, Biko is very much the strong man, and Nache stays real close, saying: 'What do you think Biko, should we go over there?' They are really good mates.

Panache is a horse that loses his confidence very easily. Never across country, where he's as brave as can be, but in the finer points of the work. In the dressage it would be very easy to destroy his confidence, and you would see it in his stride shortening up. He would get nervous and instead of getting a big, swinging, relaxed stride, his body would tighten and his steps get real short. You have to try to help a horse's temperament by bringing out the horse's good qualities. You want to be part of the solution, not part of the problem. When we first got Panache he was very nervous in the dressage. He had done a lot of foxhunting and his dressage scores were reflective of his lack of education. He had never learned how to relax in the dressage, but he always loved to jump and was really relaxed in that because that's what he had been trained to do and loved doing. He has an uncanny instinct about jumping. So we spend most of our time on the dressage because it's so much weaker with him, but we are getting there.

In our sport it is an extremely important quality that the horse can think for himself. Although the showjumping horses and riders are so articulate and seasoned at their job, in cross-country we have a real unknown factor: the terrain and the weather. Anything can happen. And it's just like a car. When you start driving faster,

> *'Horses can be inspired by their riders, but they can also become frustrated if misunderstood'*

speed involves more risk. Our sport has more margin for error because of the speed, so it is important that the horse can handle himself within the speed.

It is important not to do too much for the horse. The horse has to learn how to care for himself, but he must never be neglected. You cannot lie to the horse. You can let him do it and sort things out, but you cannot get into a situation where you put the horse in a compromising position – where he's got to stop or, because he' s courageous, he will try to jump and may fall. You don't always tell him what to do or dictate, but don't lie to him either. It is such a responsibility, but such a challenge. There is never going to be enough time in one person's life to learn everything about horses.

Partnerships are something that everybody wants, which is why I go back to the qualities you look for in a horse. You have to like a horse if you are to bring out his potential. Biko and I developed a great friendship, and though I found him difficult as a young horse, because he was so big, I always liked him and had respect for his ability. The Optimist and I never really got on. He was very strong and bullish and, again, it turned into a strength thing. I didn't feel I was really able to cope with him, and although he was very successful for me, I never got that connection with the horse's mind, which now, ten years later, is so important to me.

Horses can be inspired by their riders, but they can also become frustrated if they are misunderstood. Andrew Nicholson's ride on Cartoon II at Burghley in 1995 was unbelievable – the horse gained so much in confidence even though you never saw the rider move. He was just in a beautiful rhythm with the horse. The horse made a few mistakes and landed awkwardly, and Andrew would say 'Come, on, you're alright,' and off they would go. That was an outstanding example of a horseman with a feel of what his horse needed at that moment in time. By the end, Andrew could have convinced the horse he could jump the moon. You want to develop that quality in a horse – that he would jump off the Grand Canyon for you. However, with that trust comes a huge responsibility never to betray the horse in any way.

Whatever the discipline the horse is intended for, the trainer has two essential tasks. The first is to develop a line of communication with the horse. That changes as the horse's education goes along, so you end up with more and more words in your vocabulary. The second is to create a better athlete, and, again, this changes as the horse becomes more educated. For me, the four basic principles of any kind of riding are: straight, forward, relaxed and obedient. Straight, forward and relaxed are pretty easily explained, but obedience is a term that requires explanation because every rider chooses their own line of obedience, and it is usually relative to the discipline within their own life – what one rider will tolerate or not tolerate. As you become more experienced you find that you can take a whole string of horses and achieve the same level of obedience with exactly the same rules for all of them – that is the consistency that is so important in training horses.

To be a successful trainer you must be consistent and you must be articulate. Take any given situation, whether it's getting on a horse properly or doing a half-pass across the arena – if it is not quite right you don't just go on to the next thing, you repeat it. I cannot tell you how many times I've gotten off a horse just to get back on it better, so it stands still. It's a small quality, but when you canter down the centre line at the Olympic Games you want the horse to halt and to stand still. So you cannot ask him once out of ten times and trust that one time, by accident, he will get it right.

There is no mystery to training, it is all based on common sense. You teach the basics: straight, forward, relaxed, obedient. Then, within the basics, you make the horse a better athlete through co-ordination exercises. Then you choose the horse's career, his vocation in life – he might go barrel racing, he might go hunting, or eventing or racing, it doesn't matter. Only when you get to the very top and you think you have brought that horse to the peak of his potential, comes the point where he gets compared to someone else's horse in competition. Now the question is: 'Can you do that half-pass across the arena straight, forward, relaxed, obedient?' That's all it is. Can I go down the Beaufort Staircase straight, forward, relaxed, obedient?' It's as simple, and as complicated, as that.

Within this there is definitely an acquired skill, which is why experience is so important. You have to have a very sympathetic attitude with the horse but very direct. Keep it simple – black and white. Tell

'The biggest muscle in a horse's body is his brain. If you can get the brain to work for you, the body will follow'

the horse what you want him to do and the horse will try to do that. If he doesn't, I always look to myself and say: 'Hang on a second, he's not understanding what I am trying to say.' You may have to adapt your techniques with different horses to recreate those basics, but the basics are always the same. By all means be flexible in your methods – but you never say 'He won't do that so I'm not going to touch that, I'll leave it.'

When it comes to improving on a weak area, again it's about making it enjoyable. With Prince Panache, putting him in a 60 x 20 arena and practising dressage was not the way to go. We had to start with something he was really enjoying doing, like hacking, and use that to teach him how to accept the leg and the hand, just out in the country. When we do the jumping we ask him 'Can you do those trot-poles in shoulder-in?', or 'Do you think you could move your body this way?' He might say 'No, I don't think so.' So I say 'Come on, let's just give it a try... You see, you can do it!' The whole programme has to be very positive, so the horse then says 'Wow, I didn't realise I could do that. I could do that again. Would you like me to do it again?'

That is how you promote a horse's ability. That is when they talk back to you, their temperament is starting to come out and you are communicating. They are not shielding themselves like they do if they are worried about letting go. To get a horse to really trust, you have got to teach him how to let go of himself. Don' t protect them from the things that worry them, mentally or

physically. The most common resistances occur because a horse is misunderstood. It's a reaction. To me, the biggest muscle in a horse's body is his brain. If you can get the brain to work for you, then the body will follow. If the rider is not being understood by the horse and there is a resistance, then I would say there is a physical problem that has to be addressed – something is physically impeding the horse from doing what you want him to do. If I feel a horse does understand but he's not coming through or grabbing the right rein for example, I would call on my team – the groom, the trainer, the vet, anyone that has played a large part in that horse's progress. We would put our minds together and come up with an answer.

The horse is such a forgiving animal by nature that resistance in many cases is a man-made problem. The horse will always go to the point of least resistance. Why fight? Horses can be fighters, but in most cases they don't want a fight. Many riders come through a stage in their career when they might say that if a horse is resisting you must 'ride through it', or you get the dominance thing: 'I told that horse.' Then you find out that dominance is a matter of respect. If you fight the horse, he has lost his respect for you. That is why we have a real consistent non-aggressive attitude with our horses. That doesn't mean to say we don't ask a lot of them, but it is a non-invasive way. I almost never ride with a stick.

Resistance can also have a good quality. If a horse is resistant through a movement, maybe it's because you have taken him to

'The horse is such a forgiving animal by nature that resistance in many cases is a man-made problem'

118

the next level but you don't have the submission you need. Then you have to practise a more basic movement to create more submission, so you can then ask again, at that same standard, and have less resistance. In a particular situation, resistance is the act of asking more and not having the horse understand what you want – so it can be a good indication. Now, either at that point the horse does not understand what you want, or maybe it's not able to give what you want, or maybe it's just lazy. There are all these possibilities, and it's up to the rider to identify which one applies.

A competition horse must have a program of fitness, but there is mental preparation as well. Again, it is the management of pressure. You cannot, all of a sudden, just put a horse into a highly competitive situation, especially a Thoroughbred horse, as he will get all worked up. You must manage his mental state so he is able to do the job in hand. This applies especially in dressage where you have to have the horse precisely right – he has to be totally relaxed and confident for you to be able to go for it. If he is at all nervous, you are going to be losing points at every mark.

A happy horse is a horse that feels useful. I believe horses are workers and that they want to have a productive life. They want to be cared for and loved just like people, and to have a stability within your life and your accomplishments. So you must try to keep those qualities with the horses, and they really respond to that. Obviously the horses need to be well cared for and loved, and they must also have a routine. The rules of their life have to be consistent, as they become dependent on that.

When all is said and done, you develop the horse's personality, you have fun with him and enjoy him. Our horses do lots of tricks which they enjoy, and it makes them feel special. Horses live a lot shorter lives than we do, so you have to enjoy them now because they won't always be there. You don't just go from one great horse to another – you have to enjoy the moment. You produce each horse as an individual, to the best of your ability. If your ability will allow that horse to reach his potential, great! Then let the chips fall how they may. **'**

6 THE MIND IN TRAINING

EARLY LEARNING

Every aspect of an individual's behaviour reveals something about what he has learned during his life and how he has learnt it. Horses have an incredible capacity to learn, to learn quickly and learn well. Coupled with a natural willingness to please, this has made them extremely useful to us. But to be effective and to give the horse a fair chance of meeting our expectations, the whole process pivots around the ability of the teacher to understand his pupil and how he learns, and to set up and maintain clear lines of communication. Think how fast the horse takes on board new information in nature, when instinct and survival needs provide the ultimate motivation. His mother's smell, the location of her teats, his place in the community, how to stay upright, how to move – the lessons snowball as all the learning processes come into play like an orchestra to 'educate' the individual and shape his behaviour.

Though basic equine strategies, or patterns for living, are inherited, a young horse is not born an instant expert at these innate programmes. He needs to practise and perfect almost every life-support skill. His first and most effective trainers are his mother and the rest of the herd who, between them, teach him how to be a horse – and to be a live horse.

SOCIAL FACILITATION

Copying is central to the early learning schedule. Like all social herd-living animals, horses tend to act as a group, subconsciously 'catching' changes in behaviour from others. This tendency of activity to be infectious, called social facilitation, can be easily observed in any group of equines, a species especially prone to it. From the very beginning the young horse will tend to eat when the others in the group eat, rest when they rest, take flight when the others startle, and so on. Group action binds the herd together and provides security and stability and exerts a powerful influence on each herd member. This tendency means individual behaviour patterns are equally readily picked up. The youngster learns quickly from watching other horses, especially his mother. An old, reliable horse can be used to set a good example in handling or riding situations – but it is worth remembering the youngster can just as easily 'catch' undesirable habits as desirable ones!

LESSONS IN LIFE

Compared to a human infant the foal

A newborn foal is one of nature's fastest learners. Within hours of arrival, he is not only up on his feet but able to run with the herd.

develops in the fast lane. Within 24 hours of birth, the young foal can not only feed from the teat but be nibbling at the green stuff beneath his feet. He can move at speed, awkwardly but well enough. He can get up and lie down at will, find his own mother, call to her and she will respond. He can see off flies and has even tried out a few tentative games. As with any young animal, sleeping takes up most of the foal's time and, under the protective gaze of the mare, it is a far more relaxed affair than the adult horse's short spells of 'real' sleep. Youngsters sleep flat-out far more than older horses. As they grow, find other priorities and need to take their turn at the responsibility of 'look-out', less time is spent resting, especially in this vulnerable position. Sleep time is then mostly spent snoozing sat down or standing up using the 'locking' mechanisms in the elbows and stifles.

By watching the mare and other horses around him the foal experiments with drinking water and eating grass. Gradually the techniques are perfected. The speed and precision of the sorting and sifting process of grazing improves and the youngster learns to be able to do it almost without thinking, while keeping half an eye and ear on other aspects of its surroundings such as its closeness to the mare and the rest of the herd or any threat of danger. In social terms, above all, the real baby is a follower. Once imprinted on his own mother he will stick with her wherever she goes, frequently suckling, cementing a strong tie that in a herd situation will persist well into adulthood. As he gets a little older, however, the urge to investigate starts to take hold. This, too, is a part of the adult equine's character to a degree, as the curiosity of the horse almost matches that of the infamous cat. Unfamiliar objects are investigated using the mouth and nose or by pawing with the feet. The new foal is relatively fearless and mum has to keep a watchful eye on his inquisitive activities. Only dawning experience tells him to treat the world with less wholesale trust – then there is often conflict between his developing natural caution and the buzz of exploration.

Colts in general tend to be bolder than fillies, but all youngsters become braver and keener to range further from the mare and widen their horizons as they grow older, readying themselves for taking on independent roles. This urge is a feature we must take advantage of during the development of young domesticated horses. Making sure youngsters have plenty of opportunity to satisfy this yen to explore, so they learn about the world around them naturally and easily as they go along, can avoid the trauma inflicted on an over-protected three-year-old who is then 'thrown in at the deep end' during breaking.

Like all growing mammals, young horses love to play and need play to practise not only general locomotion but social interaction and survival skills crucial to their species. Kittens' games involve pouncing on and toying with imaginary mice. Foals play at escapes with shies,

Once imprinted on its mother, the foal will stick to her like glue. During this time she gives lessons such as body maintenance, social touching, and comfort routines like mutual grooming.

startles, turns, bucks and hasty exits. Besides sleeping and eating, most time is taken up with games of one kind or another. Improving co-ordination, sharpening up sensory perception and reactions and generally building up physical confidence are obvious functions of baby games, but among the most important of play's other roles is teaching social skills and the rules of herd living. Every encounter with another horse is an opportunity for the youngster to practise not only 'speaking' the body talk

Play and company of other youngsters helps sharpen reactions and teach physical confidence, co-ordination, social and communication skills. Research shows that foals brought up in mixed-age groups – as in the herd situation – emerge as better-balanced young adults than those who develop on their own, in pairs or in single-age groups.

that is equine language but also learning how to interpret replies. Faces, stances, noises, actions – there is a great deal of vocabulary and grammar to learn.

The young horse's status within the group is gradually altering as time goes by. At first the foal is looked upon as an extension of its mother and so long as it is happy to stay within her personal space, the status quo remains. As they get more adventurous, however, foals have to become aware of other horse's individual spaces and learn respect for their elders. The self-important adolescent two- and three-year-olds tend to take the lead in doling out discipline for any

baby behaviour that over-steps the mark. The youngster realises that even away from mother he cannot simply get his own way. He is soon put in his place in no uncertain terms within the overall hierarchy, but also has to find his niche amongst his own age-group where bold personalities soon start to boss the less confident ones. In addition, friendships and antagonisms begin to develop, both between the newcomers and between individuals of different ages, creating the complicated and ever-changing network of relationships that makes up the herd

There is evidence that demonstrates how

youngsters who grow up accustomed to herd discipline within a group with a true mix of ages, tend to be more relaxed and easy to train than those brought up in strictly single-age groups or pairs (as is the case in most western European breeding establishments). Those growing up 'nature's way' tend to be better-balanced psychologically – well-rounded individuals who are quick to learn, more 'streetwise' but respectful of fair authority and unresentful of a reprimand for unacceptable behaviour.

Weaning in the wild takes place at around nine months on the arrival of another baby. From now on, the youngsters, though retaining strong family links, are essentially on their own. Within the security of the group, however, natural weaning involves little distress compared to the trauma inflicted by the artificial, but common practice, of domestic breeders who abruptly separate mare and foal at around six months and then isolate the foal completely.

In the herd, during their yearling year, young horses like all teenagers are very much preoccupied with establishing their own identities. As one- and two-year-olds they start to lose the submissive 'mouthing' reaction to adults but are nevertheless still very much the under-dogs of the group. They are not regarded by the adults as having come of age until they are three, by which time many fillies will already have been mated, and others drifted off into new groups. Most of the colts will be in the process of leaving to create bachelor units. It may take until the age of five or six or more before the younger generation are totally

settled and established in adult roles and behaviour patterns.

The shifts in attitude that go alongside the young horse's changes in social status are significant when it comes to our handling and training schedules. Until the youngster is about three, he is essentially in 'submissive' mode – possibly ready to 'try it on', particularly if he is a bold and pushy character – but happy to accept leadership if it is convincing and clear-cut enough. From three years onwards, however, if left untouched he will become progressively less easy to influence, more self-assured and set in his ideas about his own standing.

STARTING RIGHT

The newborn foal's attitude to life is very much a blank page waiting to be written on. But the young horse learns rapidly and, in general, the younger he is when he encounters a new experience, the more affected he is going to be by it. If the rest of his life is destined to be spent in the company of human beings and conforming to our requirements, it is only fair and sensible to introduce ourselves and our 'rules of play' as soon as possible. 'Imprint' trainers exploit the newborn's overwhelming drive to associate, to learn and to look for leadership, by stamping themselves immediately on the baby's consciousness, creating a kind of *ménage a trois* where the foal looks to both mother and human for security and direction. The introduction to friendly but assertive human presence need not be quite so intrusive to still be effective. Gentle but firm handling during the first few days does

> '*The newborn foal's attitude to life is very much a blank page waiting to be written on*'

Gentle but firm handling during the first few days, when the foal is making his early judgements of the important people around him, will get the horse-human relationship off to a good start, with respect on both sides.

make a crucial impression, however, as this is when the baby is making his initial judgements about his own species identity and who are the 'important people' around him. Crouching down over the newborn foal, running the hands firmly all over the body, giving the neck and quarters a maternal-type scratch – this will all be readily accepted because the newborn is a trusting soul. In his eyes you are innocent until proved guilty

GO WITH THE FLOW

Like all training, this early presence is a form of brainwashing – of mind over matter. Even a newborn horse is far stronger than a man and allowing it any opportunity to realise this immediately puts us at a

Make use of the young foal's strong urge to follow by giving him early lessons in walking in a civilised fashion, in hand alongside the mare.

disadvantage from which it is hard to recover. The foal's species wisdom will soon set to work telling him: 'upright stance, eyes on the front of the head = alien, predator' – unless he can be conditioned into seeing human beings as non-threatening yet dominant herd members from the start. With kind but persistent handling, and the example of co-operative behaviour from his mother, he learns there is no need to resist nor indeed much point in resisting reasonable human requests. In the same way, weak or abusive treatment at this vital early stage does irreparable damage to the fragile relationship, simply confirming the strong suspicions of his instincts and

inviting him to discover how easy it can be to 'go his own way'. After this, it will be hard to convince him that resistance isn't always worth a try.

The right start can be helped along more effectively if the handler is aware at which times during growing up the youngster is particularly easily influenced because its natural tendencies lead it in a certain direction. If we go along with his own psychology, we can boost learning at the same time as avoiding unnecessary conflicts. For example, touch and smell are especially important during the early hours, and as the foal is then looking for reassurance from any large moving presence, this is the perfect opportunity to make ourselves known. During the first few weeks the baby has a strong urge to follow and is still feeling quite brave about the world, so handling is unstressful and this is an ideal time to introduce the halter and first lessons in leading alongside the mare.

The growing foal naturally starts to range, so leading and walking in-hand further and further from his dam is usually fine by him, so long as he is given a chance to weigh up new objects and experiences in his own time, as they will be treated with increasing suspicion. If the foal has not been halter-broken before, weaning is the moment to do it because the follow urge is still powerful and, additionally, the foal, feeling alone and unsure, is ready to go along with anyone who gives a reassuring lead. The yearling lives to play and explore, so will enjoy walking out and some free-schooling. Strong handling may be needed as spooking antics can get dramatic at times. Bitting could be a necessary lesson to slot in at this point, although the baby can be led in a normal halter and rope – putting pressure on the mouth ought to be an emergency resort.

At this stage although the youngster still looks naturally to a leader, he is beginning to think about testing the boundaries of this relationship and is very quick to sense when he is at an advantage. If behaviour oversteps what is acceptable, reprimands need to be as swift and decisive as in the manner that a pushy youngster would receive in the herd. The youngster is then in no doubt that it was his own action that provoked his friendly leader to change in an instant to an angry 'boss'. When horses are left to organise themselves, the younger generation start learning manners from the minute they struggle to their feet and, wobbling towards the wrong mum, get a none-too-kind shove for their pains. Discipline, so long as it is immediate, consistent and appropriate to the crime, is a positive influence that is part of life.

As he enters adolescence, the two-year-old is becoming less and less submissive, and ever more likely to test out his status at any opportunity. Now fair, consistent discipline is more important than ever. The young horse has a bright, enquiring mind and wants to be independent and see the world, so long-rein him, walk him around the place, take him to shows. He can absorb new experiences like a sponge, and as each success is notched up it will be associated with his handler's assuring presence. Keep the young horse logging new experiences all the time, with the greatest variety of situations that can be manufactured, whether they seem relevant to his future or not. The more, and the more different, chances he has to learn and to practise learning, the more skilful he is becoming at it.

Physically mature youngsters are often taken through the initial phases of backing and being sat on at the end of their two-year-old year, but most young horses, unless destined for the racecourse, are traditionally 'broken' (an unpleasant word, but familiar) when they reach three. By this time the youngster in the herd, though full of himself, is coming to realise without liking to admit it, that things don't always go your own way.

> *'As he enters adolescence the two-year-old is becoming less and less submissive'*

The two- and three-year-old wants to be independent and see the world. He can absorb new experiences like a sponge, but introduce them with care and insist fairly, but firmly, on discipline. The young horse will be testing out his status at every opportunity – and he is becoming a big strong animal

Don't get hooked on circles in the manege. To get an all-round education and develop in confidence – physical and psychological – the young horse needs get out and about in the wide world and learn that riding can be fun. An older hose as a companion helps you make use of the following instinct that remains strong until adulthood, and persists throughout life to a degree, especially in an insecure individual.

RIGHT: Learning to be ridden and to 'go correctly' is a process of complicated step-by step conditioning that takes time. With a correct, progressive conditioning schedule the horse can eventually learn complex tasks based on a barely perceptible network of clues.

BELOW: Trainers use the habituation process to build confidence by progressing towards a new lesson in small stages and going over 'safe ground' before giving a new, more demanding, request.

In the domesticated situation, if early handling has been effective the two- to three-year-old will drift into the initial stages of his education with nothing coming as a great shock. He is already accustomed to being asked questions and the to right reply being fairly but firmly insisted upon. He is learning to think, to apply old experiences to help cope with new encounters without alarm or over-reaction.

When he reaches four, five and six years old our adolescent is turning into a more mature individual, settling into adult attitudes. Now he is becoming a truly expert learner, ready for more concentrated 'lessons'. At three, however, we still have a young person on our hands who is very much a teenager in head and heart. There are going to be showdowns even in the most well-regulated households, when authority is tackled with a defiant 'Give me one good reason why!' Early handling and the initial stages of training for riding is the time when we need to set out clearly the rules of play, all the while taking into account both the animal's inborn reactions and each individual's own character. For example, is this a natural 'follower' who needs to be given confidence, or is it a leader who needs extra firmness? No approach can be rigid or inflexible – each horse is slightly different and training techniques must vary between animals.

Dialogue is taking place all the time in any situation between horse and rider or handler. Sometimes it is obvious, sometimes barely perceptible. This is where the trainer's skill and expertise as an observer come to the fore – in the ability to tell

'Any young horse can go a long way towards educating himself very effectively'

exactly when an individual is ready to be asked more and when to call it a day; when to insist and when it is best to leave matters where they are; when the horse is confused or fearful and is looking for help and reassurance, and when he understands perfectly plainly but is just being downright awkward. Bored or particularly independent youngsters sometimes put their increasing mental agility to use with some quite cunning evasions – so developing this awareness – and keeping early lessons simple but stimulating is all-important. Round and round the manege is all very well, but even in the hands of an expertly sensitive and imaginative trainer it can never foster the same outgoing confidence – or natural balance and forward-flowing energy – of the youngster who is ridden out and about in the wide world in all kinds of stimulating situations and over ever-changing terrain, and learns that riding can be fun.

Mental agility and learning capacity does vary between individuals, but what early learning illustrates is that any young horse can go a long way towards educating himself very effectively with the minimum interference and invitation to resist, if the trainer can provide three things: the right kind of environment, the right guidance, through effective communication, and the right motivation, by fostering a receptive frame of mind.

CHRISTOPHER COLDREY'S VIEW

Christopher Coldrey and his wife, Victoria, run Herringswell Bloodstock Centre, near

The Mind in Training

Newmarket, one of the most successful 'breaking' yards in the UK. Since 1981 thousands of young horses have passed through their hands on the way to winning careers, mostly on the racecourse.

'You only have to teach horses two beliefs. One is that it is easy. The other is that it is fun. If you can get that into their heads, then you should not have many problems. Only this morning we had a horse that was ridden for the first time yesterday and was quite naughty. This morning she went beautifully and after about seven or eight minutes I said okay, leave it at that, because she's done well. Tomorrow, she will remember that it was easy and it was fun.

I don't think that 'breaking' is a question of dominance in the very least, it is a question of cooperation. Horses love work. The unhappy horse is the one who is turned out in the cold field all the time, just eating grass. The happy horse is the one that is cosseted and given plenty of exercise, and who loves doing whatever he does, whether that be showjumping, eventing or hacking out.

People only climb Mount Everest because they want to, and when we ask a horse to do the equivalent of climbing Everest with us, they only do it because they want to – we would not be able to make them. The horse

**"You have to teach a horse two beliefs.
One that it is easy, the other that it is fun."**

"Driving in the long reins teaches many important things – to be in your hands, to listen to your 'legs' on their sides, and to have something around their hocks. But most important of all it makes them brave and gives them a confident attitude." Victoria Coldrey long reins a young thoroughbred.

is bigger than a human so he cannot be forced. The advantage we have is that we are cleverer, and the advantage the horse has is that he is stronger. So the only way we can succeed is by using our brains, and getting through his brain to his body. Horses have to learn respect, for your safety, but they also have to learn to love you. It is not a question of force, but of 'feel'. You simply do not have to have a row or a battle with a horse.

The system we use is a classic system of 'breaking'. Forget whether it is a racehorse or dressage horse or polo pony or showjumper, we always start them the same – it is only that the racehorses branch off the tree first. We always take the youngsters out

in long-reins and in a string of three, constantly changing the lead so they are all facing life on their own and learning to go straight. Driving in the long reins teaches them many important things: to be in your hands, to listen to your 'legs' on the sides, and to have something around their hocks. But most important of all, it makes them brave and gives them a confident attitude. I am constantly telling people that there are only three things we are trying to teach the horse at this point – to go forwards, to go straight and to go willingly – nothing else.

If a horse has never done any planned, coherent work the muscles of its back are soft, weak and unused. I believe you must build up their strength gradually by first putting on a roller and then a rug before the saddle, all over a period of time. Also, if you were to get on straightaway you would have no steering, because the horse would have no mouth! After long-reining you have a direct contact with the mouth, and to represent your legs you have had the reins on their sides. So the horses have got used to the aids for turning – the hands, legs and voice – but without the weight of the body. During the time they have been driven and lunged for a few weeks, all the correct muscles have been building up and they are strong before someone is put on them.

The most important quality a trainer must have was said by Xenophon twenty centuries ago. It was never to strike your horse in anger, and I think that is absolutely rule number one. If the horse does something wrong it is because he doesn't understand. Generally speaking, horses are very co-operative. If you do too much with them, physically or mentally, when they are young you can spoil them forever. You must only do each day as much as the horse is capable of or ready to do. At each stage the horse will tell you when he is ready to go on. So you must be patient, and you must have immense powers of concentration.

Concentration is perhaps the single biggest factor. If you are lunging a horse thinking about your overdraft, you will never get the right answer. You must concentrate all the time on what you are doing. You may only be working with that horse for an hour or so each day, but when you are with him you have to give yourself totally to that horse for that period, and try to understand what he is saying to you. Becoming a team, that is what it's all about – and if you are really good, you will become as one.

To achieve this you have to praise the horse a great deal and you must make time, because you cannot do it in a hurry. You can teach people an enormous amount, but basically you either have a 'feel' for horses or not, and you must be able to 'feel' when that horse has had enough. It's an instinct really. The 'feel' that you need to train a horse cannot be taught other than by emphasising the need for concentration, and it is not a job for a novice rider. **,**

UNDERSTANDING THE LEARNING PROCESS

Many talented horse people have produced many talented horses without the slightest inkling of the difference between a conditioned and an unconditioned reflex, or a habituated response and a habit. While feel, rather than theory, has produced the goods, the learning processes behind the success have been exactly the same.

It is easy to forget that most of what we expect a horse to learn to do is so totally alien to him that if he could laugh at the suggestions he no doubt would. Training for riding, from a horse's perspective, is more than merely pointless – it goes directly against almost every instinct evolution has drilled into him. Life with humans ought to be thoroughly confusing to a horse, and, of course, to an untrained animal it is. Training – learned experience – makes the horse/human partnership possible by gradually damping down and weakening natural objections to all these strange activities and strengthening new, learned responses to over-ride those fears. On the one hand, the process comes about through getting accustomed to the odd things we do, the situations we put the horse in, the sort of questions we ask. On the other hand, there are specific questions – when to increase pace, when to slow down, when to turn left or right – an understanding of which is arrived at by conditioning.

In either case we must remember that the untrained horse cannot read our minds. There are no natural rewards inherent in being ridden for the horse that motivate him to want to do things 'our way'. He has no conception of what our ideas of right or wrong responses are until we tell him clearly and unmistakably by our reactions, and then condition those correct responses thoroughly into his mind. Until that time he will rely on his instinctive responses – which are often far from our own notions of good behaviour! Even when education progresses to an advanced stage, the rider is still the only half of the partnership who knows the sequence of the showjumps or the movements of the dressage test. Without good communication, achieving success is like trying to win at doubles with a partner who does not know the aim of tennis or the rules. Every step towards understanding comes about through one or more of the types of learning process. Knowing exactly how these building blocks function helps avoid incorrect lessons being absorbed and impresses the right ones with maximum effect.

THE INGREDIENTS OF TRAINING

CONDITIONING: This is the principal ingredient in the recipe of training. Using conditioning involves deciding on the reaction we want to produce, creating a situation where the horse gives that reaction easily and naturally, then preceding the reaction with a precise signal so the two become associated in its mind.

What is crucial is that the lessons start with the most simple and obvious association of cue and response. Only when that is completely understood should the lesson move on to add another cue, or refine the previous one. Unless the previous lesson has been absorbed, there is no point continuing, as the pupil will only get more and more confused. Only one request should be made at a time, or our expectations can become completely unrealistic. The young horse has a great deal of vocabulary and grammar to learn – he cannot be expected to make up a sentence before he even knows his alphabet. If he is learning to halt, the halt has to be conditioned properly before fiddling around insisting on all four legs being square, or the horse's mind cannot see the wood for the trees. When he first begins to canter, set things up so that a correct strike-off is likely and stop him immediately if the response is incorrect, but if the horse does gives the wrong lead never punish him for it. Learning takes time and a full, rounded education is achieved by the unhurried, thorough absorption of small responses in the right direction.

TIMING: Correct conditioning is absolutely reliant on timing. Prompts must be immediate and consistent. Even just one badly-timed cue can at best cause a lesson to be misunderstood or ignored, and, at worst, set a wrong experience in the horse's mind.

'Habits, once established, are extremely difficult to train out, even when the original cause has gone'

REWARD: This reinforces conditioned reactions so they 'sink in', encouraging the horse to respond in the same way next time he is given the same cue. Lack of reward, or punishment, will make that response less likely to be repeated. Both reward and punishment work to strengthen the bond between a cue and the action that immediately follows it.

REPETITION: This fixes the lesson in the memory. When a connection is not regularly re-used, is no longer reinforced with reward, or is not repeated before it is fully locked-in to the long-term memory, the response becomes extinct and is forgotten. Horses, however, are particularly resistant to extinction – as good a reason as any for us to try to get everything in their training correct from the beginning.

HABITUATION: This is the principle most used in early handling and training, as it gets the horse accustomed to things that it would instinctively fear through regular exposure that has no alarming consequences. We also use the habituation process to build confidence, by progressing through lessons in small stages, allowing the horse time to accept each step fully through repetition before asking more of him. By going over an already 'safe' and familiar scenario and using that to lead into asking him to accept a further request, the horse habituates more quickly to the new demand than if he was presented with a strange challenge out of the blue. This idea is utilised by good trainers all the time, for example in laying out poles on the ground and grid work to begin a jumping lesson. With a trained horse it does have its limitations though. If you always start right back at the beginning, or spend too much of

the lesson on basics, bright horses will tend to switch off, as life is becoming too easy! The habituation principle also reminds us to keep signals sharp and intermittent and to stop the cue or reinforcement immediately the horse offers the desired reaction. Repeated over-exposure to the same stimulus can completely deaden a response.

HABIT STRENGTH: This is at work all the time, reinforcing both habituated and conditioned lessons. Guthrie's theory that a response, having once occurred, is more likely to occur again given those same circumstances than a different one, underlines the reinforcement of responses by repetition – be they good or bad. Habits, once established, are extremely difficult to 'train out', even when the original cause or connection has gone, especially if the moulding experiences became fixed some time ago. More recent experience fades quicker, but a good basis will last and always be there to build upon.

GESTALT: This the way horses tend to perceive situations. It emphasises the importance of creating the right environment for learning. Gestalt is the name given to the way that horses (and other animals) tend to respond not only to a specific prompt, but to a whole set of conditions that make up the situation at that moment in time. Depending on the combination of other stimuli that are involved, a cue from the rider or handler might be reacted on, or not. A lesson can be learnt, but in a different situation it is apparently 'forgotten' because the Gestalt is different.

Consistency of Gestalt will help fix learning, and introducing a new task in familiar surroundings provides the best chance of it being well absorbed. Altering the Gestalt, especially without warning, not only hinders learning but can help to 'undo' even well-fixed conditioned responses. This method can be useful when it comes to 'breaking' unwanted habits. Even changing one factor in a whole situation can interrupt a set learning pattern, at least temporarily, making the mind receptive to an altered perspective. The hard puller may suddenly pay much more attention to a different, milder bit. The riding school hack, deadened by years of kicking on his sides, might react to a subtle nudge.

LATENT LEARNING: Learning is known to be promoted if lessons come in short, separate bursts rather than a prolonged war of attrition. This is because rest periods allow for latent learning to take place, enabling the mind to lock-in an educative experience much more effectively. Trainers will often comment on the fact that a horse appears to have missed the point of a particular lesson completely at the time of asking, yet latched on to it immediately or very quickly next day. It is worth remembering, then, not to push any learning experience too far with the attitude the trainer 'must win or he'll be twice as bad next time'. This simply is not so in most situations. As long as the horse has been given no cause for resentment, the request was reasonable and clear and there is no 'status' confrontation involved, the chances are latent learning will ease the lesson firmly into place in its own time.

STIMULUS GENERALISATION: This occurs when a response linked with one stimulus comes to be used with another similar but not identical one. We are using this idea when we put ourselves in the position of respected leader and trusted friend in place of the herd boss or companion. The horse learns to make a broad judgement that on the evidence he has been presented with, we are a convincing substitute. Horses, being on the whole better at discriminating than generalising, can be easily upset by having to make important generalising decisions without the proper preparation. Clear and consistent signals, however refined, are appreciated. Vagueness and blurring of any kind leads quickly to confusion and apprehension, because they find it difficult to decide on what response is 'most likely' to be right. The margin for error is then wide – a situation that no prey animal can feel happy with. In a similar way, the trained showjumper or eventer copes with a whole gamut of shapes and sizes of fences, all asking different questions, largely because through experience it has reached a level of training where it can generalise, for example, that all drop fences do usually have a safe landing on the other side, even though it cannot be seen on the approach.

BALANCE REFLEXES AND BODY AWARENESS: A skilled trainer knows how to use the horse's own balance reflexes and body awareness to make learning easy by rigging up situations in which his pupil can hardly fail to do the 'right' thing, so leading on to reward and reinforcement. He uses that knowledge of how the horse moves and reacts to build up the language between horse and human that are the aids.

LEARNING THE AIDS

Horses are far more sensitive than they are generally given credit for. An animal that can feel a fly land on its skin is quite capable of responding to the minutest of signals from the rider – a slight movement of the body, the tensing of a muscle, the touch of a rein. When we use conventional aids, what is behind the way the horse reacts?

The communication system between rider and horse is based on pressure, how the horse responds to it and how he moves instinctively to re-adjust his balance when the weight on top of him shifts, however slightly. All the basic aids involve the horse reacting naturally in whatever way most easily makes himself comfortable and balanced again. Which direction the horse moves depends on the precise place the pressure is being applied, but a common misconception is that the influence of the aids is based on the horse always moving *away* from pressure. The truth is nowhere near so simple! Yes, the horse is reacting to the pressure, but not always simply to escape it. The horse's instinctive priority is to re-adjust his balance and gain relief from the discomfort he is feeling, without putting himself at further risk.

The rider's seat and body weight work as the primary signals in causing the horse to rebalance itself and so move in a certain direction. When the rider sits down more on, say, his right seatbone, the horse moves to the right because it wants to return the rider's weight to the centre of its back. When pressure is applied on one side or another, the horse moves instinctively sideways to recover his equilibrium by stepping underneath the rider's shifted centre of gravity. Schooling then consolidates this natural reaction into a conditioned response. No wonder one of the most difficult feats of

> **'Horses are far more sensitive than they are generally given credit for'**

horsemanship is to make the horse go truly straight!

Leg aids, asking for forward impulsion, also involve a natural balance reflex reaction reinforced by conditioning. Just by the girth, about mid-way between the lower edge of the saddle flap and the elbow, the intercostal nerve lies sensitively close to the surface. Any push on this nerve will provoke a spontaneous arching of the horse's lumbar vertebrae, causing him to bring the leg on that side underneath himself, so stepping forwards. In many early training schedules, the application of the leg aid to 'Go' is accompanied by someone leading the horse forwards or a click of the tongue to further encourage the association of the aids with the movement. Once the connection is well established, this additional 'help' is dropped to rely on the leg alone. Flight being his natural defence, the horse is already inclined to move forwards when he feels constricted by the rider's legs closing around his ribcage. Impulsion is produced by stimulating these instinctive reactions and then conditioning them to the aids.

Far from avoiding it, horses, in fact, tend to move into prolonged pressure wherever it is applied. This reaction is most exaggerated in any situation where the horse is tense or the pressure unyielding. Leaning on to a horse that is reluctant to pick up a foot usually results in the horse leaning back – and winning the wrestling match. The puller takes hold of the bit and bears down on it, and the worst thing the rider can do is pull back. Soft, intermittent give-and-take with both reins is needed to achieve a balanced downward transition, or on one rein, when turning, to achieve yielding flexion in the neck. If, in the turn, a wooden rein is trying to pull the head around, the horse merely stiffens against the unremitting weight on its mouth on that side. Monty Roberts has compared the horse's natural tendency to move into pressure to our own urge to bite hard to relieve nagging toothache, a similar reaction programmed into us by evolution to prevent us starving. He comments: "Nature has put that same propensity to go into pain that we have in our mouths all over the horse's body. If the horse is hurt or tense, it will move into the pain. When that dog attacks and bites into the flesh, if that horse just runs away the flesh is ripped off, the guts come out, and the dog simply sits down and waits for it to die and then has his meal. The horse that lives is the horse that goes into the pain, waiting for that fraction of a second of release, not the one that draws right away." These words touch upon the other crucial aspect of the application of the aids. When the horse has responded as required, the pressure (the aid, of whatever kind) must be eased immediately. If it is not, the horse has no way of knowing he has got it right and is allowed to stop that particular reaction. Responding easily and correctly comes naturally to a relaxed horse given the aids with precision. Emphasis and timing are what refine the fundamental structure of the language we are trying to teach the horse. His remarkable sensitivity to pressure and weight signals means that the rider's position in the saddle, bodyweight maintained in 'neutral' directly over the horse's own point of balance and then used correctly when an aid is given, is crucial if his signals are going to be clear and the horse given a chance to respond to them accurately.

SYLVIA LOCH'S VIEW

Sylvia Loch is a world authority on the art of classical riding, and on the historical breeds of the Iberian peninsula, and she has written two definitive books: The Royal Horse of Europe and Dressage *and* The Art of Classical Riding. *During a ten-year stay in Portugal Sylvia became captivated by the Lusitano horses and the elegance and precision of the Portuguese way of riding. On her return to England she established the Lusitano Stud and Equitation Centre, which became an internationally renowned centre of excellence. In 1995 she created the Classical Riding Club which aims to encourage riders at all levels with an interest in the techniques and philosophy of the classical style.*

When I went to Portugal I discovered a way of riding I didn't even know existed. Before then I had a typical country background, immersed in animals and developing the natural sensitivity which emanates from that awareness, but my riding was very hit and miss, and I didn't have a clue about dressage apart from what I had learnt at Pony Club.

I can only describe the Portuguese riders as probably being the closest thing to mounted warriors on horseback that still exist. What we read in Xenophon, in 400BC, is totally applicable to what I saw in Portugal, because although they are no longer employed in battle they do fight bulls from horseback. In the Portuguese bull-ring, which is quite different to the Spanish one, they have to prepare the horses as if the riders were going to war. The horse has to be utterly obedient to the rider. The rider cannot rely on force, coercion or punishment, because then your horse loses its natural willingness to serve, and when you are in

ABOVE: *"Impulsion should not only be forwards. The impulsion should be contained inside the rider's body, drawing the horse upwards – rather like the image of a centaur." Palomo Linares, a 22-year-old Lusitano–Arab stallion, demonstrates the piaffe, showing the roundness of the back and the poll as the highest point.*

LEFT: *"You can only teach the horse to balance around you once you, yourself, are in an extremely good posture. The rider's body puts the horse in balance, and if you get that balance the horse feels the tiniest aid." Concentration of energy and mind goes into the collected trot, as Palomo works through the back and into the rider's hand.*

Photos: T. Burlace.

such a dangerous situation, you must have a horse that wants to serve. If he is afraid of you, he will be even more afraid of the dangers you have to face. He must trust you and you must trust him.

In Portugal I learnt how to ride a horse with an understanding of gravity, something that had never occurred to me before. I had learnt the aids as one usually does – kick here, pull there, and so on – but that is completely the opposite to the way they teach. They teach the horse. From day one you have to learn that if you are not perfectly balanced and upright, the horse cannot be balanced. You can only teach the horse to balance around you once you, yourself, are in an extremely good posture. The rider's body puts the horse in balance, and if you can get that balance the horse will feel the tiniest aid. This is not an aid in the sense that the horse feels something unpleasant, like 'Kick here and he does that'. It is the opposite. You allow your weight to drop in a certain spot, and the horse will make an involuntary movement to follow where your weight is going. All the training is based on how the rider applies their weight, and the control is imperceptible.

Of course, this did not happen overnight. I went through the humiliation of thinking I could ride and suddenly I found I was useless. When I was put on a horse that was like a ballet dancer to ride, the fact I was not a ballet dancer myself but a lump sitting there, not knowing how to use my weight, made me feel utterly stupid. For the first five years I had to learn to ride again. After

that time you start to build the philosophy. I feel that even now I am only just beginning to get there, but you never stop learning. A truly great horseman is always exploring. You never get to the end of the tunnel because every horse is different, and although the principles remain the same, your approach varies with each horse.

First and foremost, the rider must learn how to be balanced over his own feet, on his own feet. If, when you are on a horse, you are not allowing gravity to come through you as you would on the ground, then you cannot affect the horse. If anything is out of synch – your head, arms, shoulders, or legs – none of the aids will work. The aids are the last part; first the rider must understand his own balance and anatomy, and get his weight correct.

Once the rider is in balance he can be made more aware of how the aids influence the horse. There is incredible ignorance of horse physiology amongst riders. When I point out to my students that the horse's longest rib is actually not under the seat of the saddle but under the twist, then they begin to realise why they must push their hips forward. The rider must learn which part of the horse's back is strongest and then learn to sit there, in balance. You also have to study the skeleton, muscles and nervous system to understand that certain parts of the horse are more sensitive than others. For example, you see people kicking away over the end of the rib-cage where there are less nerves, instead of over the longest part of the ribs.

Classical riding involves learning to ride

'Classical riding involves learning to ride the horse as he would move in nature'

the horse as he would move in nature, rather than how you think he should move. People who drive are difficult to teach classically from the beginning because they tend to steer the horse as if they were behind a wheel – they use their hands and expect the horse to go forwards into them. If the horse was in a field and moving around in flight, he wouldn't pull his shoulders round followed by his hindlegs!

The final thing is getting inside the horse's mind. Unless you are in his mind, and there is a certain feeling of love and respect and he thinks of you as herd leader, then he is never going to want to give his all to you. If he looks on you as the enemy, someone always associated with pain – even though you may feed and ride him – there is no loving cooperation and no partnership.

When it comes to training the horse, the most important principle is that nothing should ever be undone – one step must always lead to another. When you get to the top of your training tree you still incorporate all the things you did at the bottom, like a ballet dancer who still uses the five positions and all her basic training. The development of the horse comes through building all the right muscles by going through all the stages. Another basic is reward. I don't believe in punishment. I tell my horses if they are wrong by saying: 'No, I don't want that,' and they don't get patted. If they get it right, they are patted. Their 'punishment' is therefore clear: it is their lack of reward. If a horse does not go forward, I might give a stronger leg, but it is encouragement, never chastisement. If you are always fair, reward well and never punish unjustly, then even if you make a mistake they will still serve you and learn to trust you. Even horses that are totally 'brain dead' will suddenly respond if ridden with lightness. It is almost always

letting go that creates what you want rather than more force or tightness. The biggest compliment I have ever had came from a dressage judge who said that I 'never invite resistance'. I think she meant that nothing I do is likely to make the horse react against me. Perhaps she has seen too many riders putting their horse into a situation where it has no choice but to resist.

There is an obvious difference between a joyful combination, where the horse is enjoying the rider and the rider the horse, and a tense and worried, though possibly more technically 'correct', combination. The 'look at me' horse is not necessarily the one who is going soft, round and easy. It is a joy when you get both qualities, a crowd-pulling horse that also goes in a harmonious way. However, it is often the magnetic horse that is a bit anxious, and those that attract the judge's eye may not be happy inside. You see many horses doing dressage and there is nothing there. It takes an experienced judge to tell when a horse is not simply quiet but 'gone'.

Impulsion should not only be forwards. The impulsion should be contained within the rider's body, drawing the horse upwards – rather like the image of the centaur. The rider is so centred himself that the horse wants to stay under him, so is drawn upwards with the rider, **r**ather than trying to run away from him. If the horse is truly between hand and leg in the classical sense you should be able to turn from going forwards to backwards to sideways all within a second, just as you might have had to in battle to get out of danger. A truly manoeuvrable horse can do all those things, not after you have asked him but as the thought enters your mind. That is how finely balanced the horse can be. **,**

7 SETTING UP SUCCESS

For the horse to learn quickly and well, the trainer must create an environment where it is always most likely to respond correctly, making the conditioning process a natural and easy one. As horses start with the distinct disadvantage of not having a clue as to what being ridden is all about, it is only fair for us to try to stack the learning odds in their favour.

FOCUSING ATTENTION

Each response has to be fully understood and fixed before progress can be made to the next stage, but for this to happen the horse must have its full attention on what the rider is asking. The 'conversation' with the rider should ideally absorb his entire mind, with the signals of the aids becoming the stimuli that take priority in his brain. If the horse is preoccupied with other stimuli, whether they be internal feelings, say of discomfort or fear, or external sounds or sights, then lessons are not going to be learnt well.

There is absolutely no point trying to persist with teaching a horse whose attention is elsewhere, because it can only lead to frustration all round and invite resistance. Important and precise lessons that require the most focused attention from horse and rider are best tackled in a quiet

area away from the busy goings-on of the yard. Like children, young horses find concentration hard work and often unappealing. Some are worse than others, and some have more of a 'talent for languages' than others. In addition, youngsters are more easily excited, less committed to their trainer and, as yet, more weakly conditioned to doing what is asked – not a helpful combination. Learning this new language requires considerable mental effort, and to make the most of their attention span we need as few diversions as possible.

Habituation can help get a horse used to working with lots of activity going on around him, as at a show, or schooling while out on a hack. But if a horse is very distracted then it is always best to wait until he settles himself sufficiently to pay attention to his rider, rather than forcing a battle involving ever-stronger demands which are either ignored or resented and produce a whole lot of tension into the bargain. Usually it is possible to see the cause of a distraction ourselves, but sometimes it is not, so on occasions the horse appears to be being deliberately stroppy or inattentive. Here, patience is the rider's greatest gift – resisting the temptation to use more force and trying to determine exactly where the

Excess energy can be worked off in the field, on the lunge or loose schooling. Expecting a youngster full of joie de vivre to settle down to serious concentration before his exuberance has found some kind of outlet is asking for conflict.

horse's attention is being drawn. Maybe something in the far distance has caught his eye and he is, quite sensibly, slowing down to assess its danger-value. Confident, reassuring persistence is what that moment requires, not compounding the alarm by becoming domineering or, as bad, ignoring the horse's concern completely.

ENERGY TO SPARE

After an hour's work in the manege, many of us are more than happy to excuse lack of impulsion with 'he must be getting tired now'. Sometimes it may be true, but more often we are underestimating the amount of energy an averagely-fit domesticated horse has at his disposal. Forty years ago before most people owned transport, it was commonplace for a hunter to be hacked twenty or more miles to a meet, follow hounds for a full day and then hack home. Trekking ponies will trudge on at their steady pace for some six to eight hours, day after day. Even ordinary riding school mounts frequently do two or three hours active work a day at weekends without

needing a bucketful of oats to stay on their feet. Horses in the wild, at a distinct disadvantage living off poor grazing, often riddled with parasites, in foal or feeding young, still cover miles daily, including regular sprints. Even those of our horses on low-grade feedstuffs are positively buzzing with energy by comparison.

In just the same way as a child, young horses are like dynamos that have to tick, tick and tick some more until the energy level is manageable and it is reasonable to ask them to settle down and concentrate on 'school work'. The horse can be allowed to work off his excess joie de vivre either in the field, or in loose schooling or with a spell on the lunge. Again, as with children, some individuals and types have more natural fizz than others, and some are especially sensitive to other energising factors such as the state of the weather. The energy we create with feed and confinement is never going to simply evaporate if it is not allowed release. It has to find an outlet somehow, whether it be in explosive high spirits, mischief or resentment. None of these are

143

A horse that is tense is deaf to any signals from its rider. The source of tension – whether due to external factors such as activity going on around him or internal ones such as discomfort or lack of understanding – must be addressed before he is able to focus on anything other than the source of his anxiety.

very conducive to effective learning or creating an attentive, trusting rapport with the rider. The usual end result of over-exuberance is a tense, frustrated rider and a horse being punished with no comprehension why – for just feeling great and wanting to move like his nature is urging him to. Too much energy, either from over-feeding or under-work, is at the root of more behavioural problems than any other management issue.

The fact that the horse has to be reasonably calm to learn is not to say he has to be 'turned off at the mains'. To be able to receive the broadcast he has to be switched on and tuned in to the right wavelength. The trick is finding and maintaining the level of arousal which equates with optimum learning capacity, or performance, for that particular individual horse. No interest or energy blocks out learning, just as surely as too much.

KEEPING COOL

Fear, conflict, excitement – all these emotions, however they are produced, cause tension in the horse and tension is the greatest obstacle of all to learning. The 'vibes' of nervousness come across as loud and clear as a police siren to a horse. Alarming and highly infectious, they set up the expectation of trouble. As the horse will tend to react to the total situation he is in (Gestalt again) rather than a particular signal, everything about his learning environment needs to be reassuring, not only individual components in it such as the rider. The horse being prepared to go to a show knows 'something's up' by the general buzz of excitement in the air and becomes edgy and excited himself. The slightest sign of nerves or angry tension in a handler, trainer or another horse can produce fear just as readily.

When the horse is fearful or tense for any reason, it loses its sensitivity to other stimuli and so its ability to reason and keep things in proportion. In fact, it reacts in exactly the same kind of way as we do to extreme anxiety. Anyone hoping to teach and instil confidence has to learn to control tension and nervousness in their own body and replace it with an aura of calm confidence, whatever the situation.

We humans are hopeless at concealing body tension, whatever its cause. Feelings of apprehension, even if the worry has nothing to do with riding or the horse, will be transmitted like shock waves directly to an animal whose whole natural communication system is structured around the meanings of nuances of tension. The horse cannot be expected to appreciate that it is a phone call from the bank manager or a traffic jam that has made you run late, that is behind your stiff, abrupt movements or rigid muscles. He won't even equate one of his own actions – maybe a spook or a failure to respond to an aid – with the cause of your annoyance, or realise that his own fidgeting might be compounding a novice handler's nerves. All the horse knows is that tension = fear, and fear = danger. The body will instinctively ready itself for fight or flight – nothing else is important.

Everyone who rides and handles horses needs to develop an awareness of tension levels in themselves and in the horse, every moment they are in each other's company. The aim is to be as relaxed, calm and assured as possible at all times.

"The one great precept and practice in using a horse is this – never deal with him when you are in a fit of passion. A fit of passion is something that has no foresight, and so we have to rue the day when we give way to it. Consequently, when your horse shies at an object and is unwilling to go up to it, he should be shown that there is nothing fearful in it, least of all to a courageous horse like him. If this fails, touch the object yourself that seems so dreadful to him, and lead him up to it in gentleness. Compulsion and blows inspire only more fear; for when horses are all hurt

at such a time they think that what they shied at is the cause of the hurt." Sound advice from 2500 years ago, written by the Greek cavalry general Xenophon.

The fastest way to create a horse so paralysed with tension that it cannot think or act beyond its fear, is bullying 'discipline' that is excessive and inappropriate. A vicious circle of tension > resistance > hurt > fear > more tension, is instantly created and reinforced. Likewise, strapping the horse down with restrictive tackle to try and achieve a desirable outline produces a tense neck and back that are stiff and therefore insensitive to the aids.

Even a horse whose education is simply being too hurried becomes rushed and over-anxious to 'get it right' and so is going to develop a generally tense way of going. He will never have the easy air of one who is only asked for more once he has he has shown his readiness by his completely relaxed attitude to what has gone before.

EARLY WARNING SIGNS

The trainer has to become expert at spotting symptoms of tension developing in the horse and act to dispel that anxiety as quickly as possible while he still has at least part of the horse's attention.

Early warnings of low-level tension are much more subtle than the flared nostrils, rolling eyes and rigid stance of the truly terrified or angry animal. The muzzle and neck muscles are first to give the game away, producing a 'dead' rein contact. The jaw is set and the mouth dry of saliva. As mouth and neck stiffen, the whole spine quickly loses its suppleness. The horse is reluctant to flex its head and neck sideways, and forward movement becomes wooden and stilted with none of the flowing impulsion of the relaxed horse. Few horses erupt into blind panic or out-and-out defiance without building up to it with this exact series of signals, and it is up to the trainer to sense a problem situation in the making and avert it by pinpointing the cause, acting to divert a crisis and then avoid repeating the same mistake. If the horse's focus of attention shows clearly where the tension is coming from, that is one thing. But often when a horse becomes fixed in a tense attitude, the evidence points to more general anxieties about his schooling, or he is reflecting tension in the rider's body.

CARL HESTER'S VIEW

Carl Hester made a stunning entrance on to the British dressage scene in 1985 when he won the National Young Rider Championships only 18 months after first sitting on a horse. The offer of the Grand Prix rides of Dr Bechtolsteimer helped him to fulfil his early promise and led to international placings all over Europe. Carl reached the individual ride-off at the Stockholm World Equestrian Games and rode Giorgione to 16th place at the 1992 Olympics. He now runs his own yard in Gloucestershire and continues to notch up major honours at home and abroad. In 1995 he won the Pas de Deux riding Gershwin, alongside Vicky Thompson, at the European Championships.

' When it comes to searching for a horse that is going to excel in competition, mental attitude is every bit as important as ideal conformation and movement. For me, a horse has to have the basic desire to go – the will to work. There are many things you can pick up on when you are trying horses temperament-wise. Obviously, all young horses are going to look at things, but do you get the feeling that you are going to have to ride this one past something twenty times and it will get worse and worse, or is it the kind that, if you allow it to look, it will go past and learn for next time? Even in a very young horse, I would not want him to be resentful of being squeezed with the leg or taking up a contact.

Presence is what distinguishes a horse that will make it right to the top. It does not necessarily need to be good-looking – its presence can make it beautiful. And I am sure the top horses do see their tests as a kind of performance. The horse I rode at Barcelona, Giorgione, was very talented but, at home, you could imagine him putting his hoof to his mouth and yawning, he was so lazy. Yet, at a show, that horse was magnificent. I had to ride so, so quietly because he was loving it so much; he carried me through tests. I had to learn to relax about the fact that he would go so badly at home, because when we went somewhere he would go 'Yippee, look at me!'

It isn't true that the dressage horse has to be a quiet dog. The best of them are electric horses, because when you reach Grand Prix level if you haven't got a sharp, keen horse, you cannot have that edge. Dressage is no different to eventing or showjumping, where, if you haven't got a horse that takes you to the fence wanting to jump, you are not going to make it to the other side. You can force anything up to a point, but when you get to Grand Prix level, the difference between the ones being made to do it and those doing it for themselves is plain to see. Their collection is natural.

A dressage horse does not need to be super-intelligent, but he does need to be allowed to have initiative. If all his instincts are taken away by over-dominance in training, always making the horse obedient and fixed on the bit, that is when you lose

"I don't think you can ever develop a partnership if you are in a 'factory' situation where someone gets your horse ready, you get on, and that's the last you see of him until next time." Carl Hester at home with two rising young stars.

the sparkle that makes the very top horses. Dressage can easily become too regimented. You can go to a sale in Germany and see 50 young horses with beautiful movement, yet the majority will not reach competition level. Something goes wrong somewhere along the line. I think the reason so many fall by the wayside is that the system is so regimented their temperaments don't last. Dressage work is, has to be, the same all the time, because it is repetition that the horse learns from. But the horse must have relief and variety. We are fortunate here in that we are able to go out for a hack to do something different when we want, or need to.

I think if horses are trained in a

progressive scale, they enjoy learning and they enjoy using their bodies. If you can make your training a black and white system, praising the horse when he does well, then he will look for praise. If he makes a mistake you stop, correct him and do it again, then he understands. Things go wrong when they fall into a grey area. For example, a rider holding on to a horse that pulls, creates more and more of a block. You must give time to your training so you can play and be flexible, and you must be creative enough to try different things so it stays varied.

You must always remember that to make a horse supple, whether it be laterally or over the top, you cannot keep them in the same outline all the time. We work a lot on changing the outline, stretching the top, collecting, bending and straightening, until the young horses learn they must never be fixed in one place but always must be moving. I work on the premise that you need to be doing 100 to 150 transitions during every schooling session. It is so important not to keep on with things that are not working. If the horse does not canter well, it is no good to keep him cantering. It is going through trot to canter, or trot to walk or whatever you are working on that is going to activate the quarters, not working in one pace. We work a lot with trotting poles, again finding different ways of relaxing the horses and stretching their backs.

You can put the worst mover in the world in a field, and if something was to excite him, you could see ten times the movement from him that any rider could ever achieve with that horse. What happens when a rider gets on the horse's back is his whole balance changes. That is what can be corrected and helped to develop, but only through years of strengthening the horse, balancing the horse, teaching the basics and carrying them all the way through. As they go up the ladder, many horses become bogged down in doing the movements. Riders start riding stronger or rougher because they are concentrating so hard on this advanced work and the next competition. The overall light picture is completely lost.

A tight body comes out of a tight mental state. I work with a lot of event riders with extremely fit horses, and all we have to work on is relaxing them. When the mental is relaxed, the physical is relaxed. Many trainers used to think you cannot expect to do advanced movements without tension – that you needed the nervous energy to produce the movement. Then Reiner Klimke came along and showed there was a different way, as his horses were never tense.

Dressage is a difficult sport, because the mental demands upon a horse in an arena are a great strain. His natural instincts are those of a flight animal, yet here he is surrounded by tents, flowerpots, judges in boxes, huge crowds moving in the stands... To retain the horse's concentration with no

"The horse I rode at Barcelona, Giorgione, was very talented at home, but so lazy. Yet, at a show, that horse was magnificent. I had to ride so, so quietly because he was loving it so much; he carried me through the tests."

tension whatsoever takes quite some temperament. Channelling their energy is mainly in the training and getting to know how much you can let the horse out, how much it needs working in, and being able to trust it enough that you don't exhaust it before you go in and so produce a dull performance. All this comes from assessing the horse and getting to know it. Unfortunately there are very few horses that are harmonious with their riders and who look tension-free. Many riders sit beautifully, but win with tense horses. It is the feeling with the horse that makes you truly talented.

Too often, insufficient time is spent on developing the basics – the paces and balance – then the movements are attempted before the horse is physically capable or mentally ready. The situation we have in the UK is unfortunate in some ways but fortunate in others. Dressage is an expensive sport and we don't have an endless stream of horses here. Therefore most people persevere and try a different approach if problems arise.

A classic case of this was Emile Faurie's Virtu. That was a very switched-off, non-forward-thinking horse until Emile spent time with him and began training him out on the gallops. Suddenly the horse could look ahead and think of doing other things beyond the school. It worked, and he came away with a European bronze medal. It is a lot about being open-minded. Gershwin, for example, at the beginning of the year wouldn't go near anything that frightened him, or even into his corners. You tend to start off thinking 'He will go near it', in a

forceful kind of way. But as we got a partnership together, I realised in fact he was very, very nervous and then I began to ride him differently. At home he works beautifully, happy and relaxed now, but still when he gets into an arena he becomes a solid plank of wood. It is so frustrating that you feel like getting a hold of him and making him do it because you know that he can. But what I had to learn to do with him was forget the competition and give the horse a chance. If he wanted to look at something I found he actually relaxed more quickly if I let him look and just kept going around steadily, than if I held on to him.

It's a case of taking every horse as an individual, seeing how you can best take away that horse's tensions, and making sure there is enough time in the day to finish a job properly. Lunging, long-reining, gridwork, poles, hacking, schooling – always look for what that horse really needs instead of looking all the time for what will make him subservient.

> *'It's a case of taking every horse as an individual, seeing how you can best take away tensions'*

I don't think you can ever develop a real partnership if you are in a 'factory' situation, where someone else gets the horse ready and you get on, then off, and that's the last you see of him until next time. You need to have time with the horse in the stable. At top level this is such a strenuous, demanding sport, both physically and mentally, you must be completely involved and know the whole horse.

One of the best partnerships I have had was with a young horse called Boucheron. As I didn't have many other horses when he came to me, I had the chance to be with him and not to be in a hurry. I had to try many

149

different things to find the key to him so he would allow himself to be ridden without taking away his character, which was naturally expressive and forward-going. He wanted to explode, so if you over-reacted that was that – it all fell apart. I was the only person who ever rode him, and he went on to become national champion at two levels.

Another example is Nicole Uphoff and Rembrandt. That is a hot, spooky horse, but you never see Nicole lose her patience with him. She moves with him whatever he does. At home she spends a lot of time with him, grooming him and hacking him out herself. The first Grand Prix Rembrandt competed in, he came last, but with Nicole's patience, going along with him and trying different methods, she has developed a partnership that has been the most successful in modern dressage.

To create a good partnership there must be trust, so you must be consistent. Why ride the horse differently in the arena to the way you do at home, for example? That is the kind of thing that breaks down trust, that and falling into the trap of wanting perfection every day, all of the time. Yes, of course we are aiming for perfection, but on your way you must not be constantly changing your mind, confusing the horse.

I would like to be able to train a horse to look like an effortless dancer at that highest level. In my own personal training, I would like to break down those barriers that make so many horses look tense. When I was young and ambitious I wasn't into dressage as an art form, because I didn't know

enough. I was going for the team, which makes you train differently, ride differently and push horses. But there is so much to be learned and now my own challenges lie somewhere else.

Once you have ridden a horse that is well trained in a pure way, there is nothing like it. I never thought that dressage could keep me going or that the adrenalin would stay, but it has. Some of the adrenalin for me comes from competition, but most comes from the horse himself. These top horses are something else to ride, with their lightness and energy. That is the challenge for me now, to create that overall picture of the rider and the horse, together. **'**

DEVELOPING A SENSE OF TIMING

Getting the timing right can make all the difference to learning in various ways. As we have seen, the introduction of new tasks at the optimum stage in the horse's life gives him a helping hand because we are making our requests at a time in his development when his natural inclinations are taking him along that road anyway. So he is happy and willing to oblige. The timing of specific lessons when the horse is in a receptive state of mind can determine whether he is quick on the uptake or completely ignores a request, rapidly leading to frayed tempers all round. Not being 'in a listening mood' could be due to a general feeling of uncooperativeness on the day, like the mare who is in season or the over-exuberant youngster kicking up his heels on a fresh, windy morning. It could be because

'A punishment applied even one minute after the crime is a minute too late'

attention is temporarily diverted, or that he is being asked too much, has not understood, is physically tired or unbalanced and so unable to do as we ask, or there is tension in the body for whatever reason. To insist on hammering home a lesson under any of these circumstances is a sure way of inviting confrontation or resentment and further lack of co-operation. Humans never learn well when not in the mood and we object to being pushed at those times. Horses are no different and it is the trainer's responsibility to know whether to 'call it a day' or if it is worth trying to boost motivation by creating a better mood, for example by changing the situation slightly (altering the Gestalt).

Incorrect conditioning – the failure to understand or the unwitting reinforcement of the wrong reaction – is at the root of most training and handling difficulties. Any fresh lesson that has not been prepared for fully by completely conditioning the previous step is also badly timed and setting up a likelihood of failure. Focusing in closest of all, the timing of the actual cue or aid at the precise moment when it is most likely to produce the correct response is crucial. This can be the matter of a split second. The skill that it takes to judge that right moment, and to be physically able to give the right cue at that instant, takes years and years of practice, as well as an instinctive 'feel'. Training a horse well does take a very good rider, someone who is quick thinking, able to concentrate hard, and in complete control of his body and its reactions.

The knack is to be able to give the prompt to the horse just at the moment when he was about to do that movement, or a very similar one, anyway. That movement can then be paired with an aid, reinforced by reward and repetition, until the aid becomes the signal for the movement. Asking for

canter just as the outside hind leg comes underneath the body to encourage the correct lead, saying a soothing 'Walking...' as the horse on the lunge is slowing slightly, about to fall into walk – conditioning connections must be linked by one or two seconds, no more. The trainer has to be able to feel or see what the horse is intending to do in the next instant if he is trying to condition an action to a signal effectively.

Timing of discipline follows the same

It is already too late to 'punish' this horse for refusing. By the time he has turned away and the rider has organised herself to use the whip, his mental association of the two events will already be lost.

principle. Physical punishment is known to be ineffective with horses because it is a tension and fear creator which blocks out positive learning. Punishment in training is a bad idea for other logical reasons. For a start, it is singularly useless as a reinforcer of a response because it generally happens after the event. A punishment applied even one minute after the crime is a minute too late, because there will be no connection whatsoever made in the horse's mind between the two actions. It means absolutely nothing more to the horse than that he is being beaten for no apparent reason – or for whatever he happens to be doing at that precise moment. A horse whipped as he jumps a fence, in an attempt to get him to pick his feet up higher, is being punished for jumping. Being jagged in the mouth by a disgruntled rider who gets on after being bucked off tells the horse that being mounted is suddenly a painful experience – not that he should not have bucked five minutes previously. Chastising the horse you have just managed to catch after he has led you a merry dance around the field for the past hour does nothing more than confirm to him how right he was to avoid you in the first place.

Punishment can be used in learning if we are attentive enough to the body language that warns us of the horse's intentions. It can prevent mischief of a horse's own making by intervening before he completes an unwanted reaction. A horse pulls a face to bite so gets a growl in response, or arches his back to buck and receives a smart smack behind the girth that drives him instantly forwards. This kind of 'self-inflicted'

> *'We tend to take for granted that when given an instruction the horse understands it'*

discipline prevents any link being formed between unpleasantness and the rider. It is the undesirable action which is directly connected with the unpleasant consequences. If administered instantly, on the threat of trouble, such discipline often only needs to be mild and can pre-empt real problems developing.

SIGN LANGUAGE

Riding is a dialogue. Reading the signs – of timing, of tension – this is what creating the environment for learning is about. It is not enough to send out signals; the trainer has to be able to receive them too. Any form of communication involves not only knowing the meaning of the 'words' and being able to 'speak' them, but also interpreting the responses that come back.

The horse is communicating with us all the time, giving us all the evidence we need about how he is feeling, what's bothering him, if he has understood what we are asking, if he's happy with it, relaxed and ready for more. His one biggest problem is that we are generally so intent on trying to talk to him (or usually, shout at him) in our language, that we are never quiet enough for long enough to listen to his reply. In many cases, that feedback might be that he is totally failing to comprehend what we are talking about, or that our signals are inconsistent, sending conflicting, confusing messages. We tend to take for granted that when we give an instruction the horse understands it, and if he fails to respond as we intended we arrogantly assume he is being deliberately evasive. With so little common ground on which to go forward, progress halts and uncertainty takes over. Misunderstanding crystallises into fear and objections.

Often the problem lies in us being so preoccupied with the linguistic mechanics – sit up straight, shoulders back, feel the left rein now to turn left, putting the right leg back a little behind the girth, left shoulder back, look between the horse's ears – we completely miss the dialogue, often very complex and subtle, that is a continuous background music between us and the horse. The least we can do is acknowledge we have heard that the horse is making a comment, even if, having used our judgement, we then decide to insist he responds as we asked and give another, more definite and unmistakable aid or signal. Only when a horse is thoroughly trained in our language and we are as sensitive to his – all of which takes many years – can a real relationship of mutual trust and respect be established where horse and man are equal partners.

REINFORCEMENT

What makes a horse more likely to repeat an action? To teach effectively – that is to condition our signals thoroughly with the responses we want to produce – we have to master the art of knowing when, how much and what kind of reinforcement is required. Reinforcement loads the odds on the horse doing the same thing next time he is asked the same question, or, in the case of an unwanted action, not doing the same thing. It can either be positive, encouraging the repeat of the response, or negative, discouraging it.

POSITIVE REINFORCEMENT: This comes in the form of a meaningful reward that is given either during the action or straight afterwards, motivating the repetition of that action if the same cue is given. Horses love to be praised, and not necessarily by being given a tidbit, though this is always appreciated momentarily. A scratch on the neck or word in a kind, reassuring or encouraging tone is equally meaningful, if not more so, as it is a natural way for a horse to show and receive appreciation and friendly 'vibes'. Cessation of a stimulus can be reward enough to achieve conditioning – the release of pressure on the bit as the horse slows, or stillness of the heel after a leg aid is responded to. It is also possible to condition an action to become a reward in itself. The horse who enjoys jumping will consider it a reward to spend ten minutes popping over a few fences after a taxing session of flat work. Most effective in motivating the horse to want to please and to go along with his rider, whatever the circumstances, is the sense of appreciation and improved communication that liberal doses of praise will bring. It is remarkable how many horses go on giving their best for riders who are slow to reward their effort, but hasty to punish the slightest error.

During the early stages of learning, when a signal is first given, it might provoke any of several different responses. The rider who makes a good trainer needs to be patient and wait for trial and error to tell the horse which is the 'right' one. Learning will happen only if reward comes for that correct response alone. It must also come consistently, every time the correct response is given. This is not such an easy task for the rider as it might sound and requires quite a feat of concentration. Later, when that response is conditioned, the reward is more effective if it becomes partial, to prevent the horse becoming habituated to it. A horse learning the preliminary stages of lateral work can be praised for a little sideways movement. A more advanced horse is better motivated by the appreciation of a complete half-pass well done.

Rewards are one way of increasing motivation, and bribes, where the horse sees promise of future reward, are another. The youngster reluctant to jump may pluck up the courage if he can see his friend on the other side. The one teetering on the edge of the trailer ramp could just be persuaded to put a foot on if he was hungry and a bucket of food is sighted at the top. Bribes are most effective when they utilise one of the horse's natural urges, but, even then, much depends on the individual horse and circumstances. If the drive for food or company is strong, such a bribe might work well. If he has just fed or his worry is so great he would rather not jump, no matter who is on the other side, then the chances are that no amount of bribery will shake his resolve.

NEGATIVE REINFORCEMENT: An association can also be reinforced negatively, the reinforcement either actively discouraging the action it is linked with or teaching the horse to avoid potential unpleasantness. As we have already seen, punishment is not a very effective reinforcement because, more often than not, it occurs too late. Punishment can eliminate a response if it comes instantly, so that there is some kind of linkage in the horse's mind between two events, but even this effect is generally short-lived. Scientific research has demonstrated that in the long term even harsh punishment does not over-ride the urge to repeat 'old learning'.

When a punishment is used for an action that is not performed, there are pitfalls, even when it is given instantly. The horse refuses a jump and the rider is certain that it was not due to communication difficulties – the horse should have taken off. He smacks the horse immediately so that it should make a connection between 'crime' and punishment. Hopefully, the horse is discouraged from repeating the stop and, at the same time, encouraged to take off next time. The absence of a smack when he does take off positively reinforces the act of jumping. Giving this smack, however, can be a dicey business. For a start, the punishment must come lightning-fast – and how many riders are that quick? Secondly, it must happen while the horse is still stood directly in front of the jump. Once he is turned away, on the one hand the turn rewards him for saying 'No' , and on the other, if he is then smacked, he is being punished for the turn and not for the stop. Now he is completely confused! In addition, studies have shown that, following punishment for not doing something, an action might subsequently be performed but is done grudgingly, with the minimum effort. Is that going to produce a successful performer who enjoys his work?

There are many good reasons why the use of active punishment is a minefield best avoided, but perhaps the simplest and best of all, from any trainer's point of view, is that it is counter-productive and a singularly ineffective method of reinforcing an association. After all, why should the

'There are many good reasons why the use of active punishment is a minefield best avoided'

horse have got it wrong? A relaxed, attentive horse, given correct aids at the correct moment, will almost always make a try at the correct response, even though it might not be as spot-on as the rider hoped. Poor preparation, distractions, bad timing, a fuzzy prompt or tension produce 'mistakes' – and whose fault are they? This is not to say that disobediences don't happen and that persistence and firmness are not necessary at times, even regularly, with strong-minded individuals. Horses are by no means all saints, desperate to please us out of affection and loyalty. What they do respond to is being firmly and fairly treated, and on these terms they are more than happy to build up a rapport, but one based on respect rather than fear.

Many resistances are a reaction to lack of understanding or another breakdown in communication. The horse cannot escape the situation, so it fights – it resists. The rider needs to learn to be able to distinguish defiance from confusion or anxiety.

STEPHEN HADLEY'S VIEW

A former international showjumper, Stephen Hadley is now a top-level trainer and television commentator. He was a regular member of the Nations Cups teams throughout the 1970s, chalking up a string of international honours before turning his attention to teaching in the 1980s. His training yard now draws eventing and showjumping riders of all levels, and Stephen travels widely as trainer of the British Young Riders team. He is a member of the BJSA's Executive, Training and International Selection committees.

 Showjumping, eventing and dressage are all taxing on a horse's mind and body at top level. For all three disciplines horses have to have a good mind or they won't stand the training. You can tell the kind of attitude a horse has by the time it is four years old.

As soon as a horse is broken and riding we begin putting him over poles straightaway. I believe in finding out if a horse has got the ability and if he is temperamentally suited to the job early in his life rather than wasting a year or two then finding out he's no good.

The top of my list, the first thing I go for – either when buying a horse or trying to breed a horse – has to be conformation. Although this would appear to have nothing to do with the mind of the horse, it is important because correct conformation enables a horse to do his job so much better than faulty conformation. Not only that, but if a horse is well made it is almost always better balanced; it is therefore easier to train because the horse finds everything easier, and will stay sounder for longer. Pedigree is important too. There's an old saying among horse breeders: 'the apples don't fall very far from the tree', and that applies to soundness and temperament.

After conformation, I look at a horse's attitude which I can tell by the look in his eye, his facial expression, the way he reacts in any given situation. A nice horse will look you straight in the eye. He tends to think what he's doing; he will look after himself and he will look after the rider at the same time.

If a horse is well-bred and well-ridden he can usually jump a decent fence by the time he is four, and then it is a case of really learning the job and adding a bit more technique. With an over-brave horse you are working on bringing him back all the time, whereas with a timid horse you are driving them on. It's like having a median point that

"Sunorra would have just pulled up if I had stopped riding her because she was so timid – she was careful. You need a perfect balance between the 'chicken' and the brave. If there's too much 'chicken' you won't jump a big combination because they won't have the guts to do it. Too much bravery and they will never jump a clear round."

Photo: Bob Langrish.

you are trying to reach all the time, getting them to the right cruising speed.

Temperament certainly is half the battle with showjumpers. I have worked a lot with Mary King and her horse, King William. He can gallop across country, he has loads of stamina and power, he's a great mover – but he is not a natural showjumper. Because he finds it difficult it worries him, and because he doesn't have the easiest mind in the world he can blow up. At international level where the showjumping in the three-day event comes last he will have four or five down, compared to one-day events which he wins like shelling peas, because he showjumps early in the morning when no one is there.

A good showjumping horse does know that he's aiming to jump clean. They don't like to knock the fence and they don't like hurting themselves. The good ones find it easier to clear the fence than knock it, and prefer to

John Whitaker and the great Milton. "Top horses have lots of ingredients – ability, technique, a good mind, conformation. It is equally a case of being able to do it and wanting to do it."

do that. Those ones only tend to have a fence down through inaccuracy, not usually because they don't care. If a good horse knocks a fence he won't hit the next one because he knows they are there to be jumped. It's unfortunate that the good ones do more work than the bad ones because they are always jumping clear rounds and so going twice; they're their own worst enemies really! The four-faulters only do half the job, and half the work in a lifetime.

Good horses are looking for the next fence when they have jumped one. Some horses are quite ambitious and like to get on with it and really take you to a fence. I used to jump an old horse called Corunna Bay in puissances and he won a few. When he turned the corner at Wembley or Olympia or wherever and saw that big wall, he would tow me all the way down to it, he so wanted to go and jump it.

The best horses I have had have all had

very different characters: some laid-back, some hyper, some a bit timid, some over-brave like Corunna Bay going at that wall. But in contrast, another good horse I had called Sunorra would have just pulled up if I stopped riding her, it was as simple as that. Because she was timid, she was careful. You need a perfect balance between the 'chicken' and the brave. If there's too much 'chicken', then they won't jump a big combination because they won't have the guts to do it. Too much bravery and they will never jump a clear round, because they will be taking the fences on too much.

Clearing the fences involves a combination of the horse's ability and the rider's ability. The top rider will put a horse on a spot, from an approach, from which it is easier for that horse to jump that fence clean than to knock it down. They have the horse in such a good outline, in front of the leg, between the leg and the fence, on such a spot that the horse will take off and make the best possible rounded bascule over the fence. Consequently, in 19 cases out of 20, if the horse is a clean jumper, it is more inconvenient to knock it down than jump clean. It is all about making it easier for them. However much a horse wants to try to jump fences, if he has not got a natural technique then he is going to have fences down. If he is a natural jumper with a brilliant rider, and he's got scope, and what you are asking him to do is well within his abilities, you can count the number of fences he's going to have down in one season on one hand.

A showjumper definitely has to be more on the side of super-clever than super-obedient. A horse who is merely obedient is very dependent on who is sitting on his back. A clever horse can look after himself and help the rider out a bit. If you have a totally obedient horse with a super rider on his back he is never going to have to be clever, and never going to get into the situation where he's got to learn what to do if the rider makes a mistake. There is not any one factor that marks those who will make it to the very top. Top horses have a lot of ingredients: ability; technique; a good mind; conformation. It is equally a case of being able to do it and wanting to do it. And when they want to do it, they are good at it and find it easy and so enjoy it. It's all about confidence.

Twenty years ago the job was much less demanding. Courses are much bigger and more exacting these days. Half of the horses of 30 or 40 years ago would not get past the third fence today – they just couldn't get the distances or do the gallop. Even when the horse himself is a perfect candidate, trust and confidence in the rider is all-important, and a great deal hinges on the rider's ability. The horse and rider have got to like each other. Some horses can be good, but you don't necessarily like them. The horses I have done best with tend to be the nice, capable, quality horses that are happy to give of themselves as much as they can. They have almost become personal friends. **,**

AVOIDANCE CONDITIONING
Trainers that are proud of never, or rarely, using active, physical punishment often still base their system on avoidance, the principle behind much of conventional training. The horse moves forward at the slightest pressure from the heel because it has learnt that if it does not a harder aid will follow, quite possibly backed up by the whip or spur. Whether this is necessary or desirable is questionable, as we know how easily worry leads to tension and all that

that entails. Plenty of positive reinforcement, with mistakes ignored and a task repeated, produces an alert horse that is genuinely willing, not in constant fear of not reacting correctly. As with punishment, insistence on avoidance conditioning can lead to the horse continuing to react but 'under duress', even carrying on when it is uncomfortable or unhappy because it is afraid to object or stop. Xenophon comments: "It is the best of lessons if a horse gets a season of repose whenever he has behaved to a rider's satisfaction. For what a horse does under compulsion...he does without understanding; and there is no beauty in it either, any more than if one should whip and spur a dancer."

A horse scared of making the slightest mistake, especially when he is unsure of what is expected of him, is never going to be natural and expressive in his movements, willing to put himself out for his rider or even half-reliable in a difficult situation. For the horse trained with praise and reward, any stiffness in his rider's body or rough tone of voice is quite enough to transmit disapproval when it is needed. The horse looks to the 'feel' of his rider to tell him if he has made a 'right' or 'wrong' response. Aversion training can certainly create an obedient horse, but the respect for the rider will then be based on dominance rather than on a true partnership of co-operation and understanding between two species. The submissive horse will do the bare minimum and, in the face of any demanding test, the relationship is unlikely to stand the strain. When it comes to the crunch, fear, flight and

fight will almost certainly take over. If the result of that is yet more punishment, more often than not, the animal throws in the towel altogether on this confusing, soul-destroying business of trying to communicate and becomes an automaton, all thoughts turned on how to avoid further pain. An obedient horse is not necessarily a cowed horse, though. He can be obedient because he understands precisely what is being asked of him and is doing it either to gain his reward or avoid punishment. This situation sounds good – but it still implies a very one-sided conversation. It is learning by rote, the horse's whole concentration focused on each command and whether he is making a right or wrong response. The rider is the drill-master on whom everything depends. A better perspective is to look at the way the language itself is being 'spoken' and how the horse is interpreting it and replying to it. If signals are being put across clearly and the horse is responding as the rider wishes, then communication is being effective and successful. If there is a hiccup in communication and the response is not forthcoming, let's discover where the breakdown occurred. The horse himself will often provide all the clues in his own 'lingo'. Now the conversation becomes a true dialogue with room for personality and self-expression, with neither side feeling threatened or under stress. The horse is given room to think about what it is doing and be at ease with it. Horses are good at conversation, it comes naturally to them. They are far too sensitive to need dominating into obedience, and if they are,

'*A horse scared of making the slightest mistake is never going to be natural in his movements*' what is reflected on the trainer speaks for itself. Xenophon writes: "And in everything else, as I have insisted over and over again, the horse should be well rewarded as long as he behaves well. When you see a horse show his pleasure by carrying his neck high and yielding to the hand, there is no need of harsh measures as though you were forcing him to work; he should rather be coaxed on, as when you wish him to rest. He will then go forward cheerfully to his swift paces.

"When he is induced by a man to put on all the airs and graces which he puts on of himself when he is showing off voluntarily, the result is a horse that likes to be ridden, that presents a magnificent sight, that looks alert, that is the observed of all observers."

MARY KING'S VIEW

Mary King has been a regular member of the British three-day event team since 1991, with the ebullient King William, just one of a string of talented performers that she has produced to international level. Her enthusiasm, dedication and commitment have made her a popular ambassador for the sport of eventing, and she has been rewarded by successes such as Badminton 1992, team gold and individual fourth at the 1994 World Equestrian Games, and team gold and individual bronze at the 1995 European Championships.

'You can have a horse that has got all the ability in the world – the movement, the jump – but if the temperament isn't right that horse will never be consistent at top level. I have felt certain about the horses that have proved to be the most successful from the very first moment – you look in the stable and get that feeling. As soon as I saw King William, I said 'Yes! There's something about him.' It was just the way he stood there, his general outlook was so positive. Even the way he would walk out of his stable was purposeful; the way he trotted up in-hand. He was so obviously a forward-thinking horse, alert in his mind, and that really appealed to me.

I have had some horses that were ever so calm and relaxed when they were young, and I thought they had a lovely temperament. They roll along quite easily, but sometimes they turn out to be quiet because they are not that intelligent. If they are very calm, maybe they are a bit 'thick', so when you start asking for more and more, their mind can't quite keep up with it all. So a good horse does need to be a bit sharp and intelligent and gritty. The ones that are very calm when they are young may not have that grit and determination.

In terms of obedience, that depends largely on how accurate a rider you are. If you are very accurate you can get on with horses that are purely obedient, but the ones that just do what they are asked cannot work it out for themselves if you run into trouble, whereas the cocky and headstrong ones think for themselves. That is, as long as you can channel all that, as it often comes out as naughtiness when they are young. You have to channel that energy into working with you as a rider. Then, if you make a mistake in an approach to a fence and it's going wrong, the horse will get you out of it.

Showjumpers have to be more obedient than event horses, as it is much more of a mechanical sport. They are going out every day doing exactly the same thing, and for some horses that would not be enough. A top showjumper is an absolute freak, he has to be consistently so careful, actually wanting not to touch the fence, and doing everything he can not to touch it. For our sport that would be hopeless, because when you are jumping big drop fences a horse who took so much care would end up injuring himself all the time. Often the top showjumpers are so careful they would not be brave enough to do our sport, where they really have to gallop at jumps – it would go against the grain compared to eventers who have to be rougher and tougher. Showjumpers are a bit precious in a way, which is what makes them so brilliant. We eventers almost encourage our horses to be a bit naughty and think for themselves, to be street-wise.

There are many little ways you can encourage a horse to think for himself. Turning out certainly keeps their minds active, and when we come back from a ride, for example, our horses all have to stand on their own in the yard while we go to get the headcollars. When we are mucking out and grooming, they must stand without being tied. These are just little ways where they have to use their brains and work out what is expected of them. They have a choice and must make a decision, rather than being so regimented they never have to think. You have to trust your horse as much as possible.

A horse must be enjoying himself to be successful, whatever he is doing. He must be giving his all. I have had horses that have reached a certain stage and they are clearly not going to make eventers; they would be better at something else. You often see riders persisting with horses that just have not got the scope, or the will to want to do it. You see riders going on and on with these horses, doing round after round, and they are never going to be good enough to reach the top – it is not the horse's fault, it is just

> '*A horse must be enjoying himself to be successful, whatever he is doing*'

the way he is made. I try to make up my mind as soon as I can, rather than persisting with a horse that either cannot do it easily or doesn't enjoy it. Horses that don't really enjoy it might be fairly successful, but they are doing it because you are asking them, and they have been taught to obey. There is no enthusiasm there, and enthusiasm is your clue to their potential.

King Boris, who has just retired, was not really an event horse stamp at all; he is quite chunky with the stamp of a three-quarter-bred horse, so he found the galloping and speed needed at top-level competition quite difficult. He was only so successful because he had such a big heart. All through his life he wanted to please you. Whenever I ran into trouble, he just did everything he possibly could to jump that fence. Boris might not have been the most talented horse, but he just had that big heart and the will to want to help you and to do it right. He was so good in his mind and, after years of training, so obedient. He had to try every inch of the way, but he was so genuine that he was immensely successful.

Then, you get the other extreme of King William, who is just so naturally talented that it is easy for him to do. He could gallop for miles, and has got lovely movement and presence for dressage. He was almost too forward-thinking as a young horse and too headstrong. It was a matter of getting him to settle and wait, and be calm, whereas with Boris you were always revving him up. However, problems have arisen with William because he is so talented, because of the way his mind works, especially in the showjumping phase. With a big crowd and a tense atmosphere, he just loses his mind and can't focus on the jumps at all. They are not that big, and he knows he can jump them easily. When he is calm at home, or goes to little events, he will jump endless clear rounds. But when he's in a tense atmosphere, he gets concerned, and that is when he will start to knock fences down. Some horses seem to respond to that kind of atmosphere in a competition and love it, but William is very, very sensitive to that tension.

He is not the show-off sort of horse that people tend to think he is. When you see him at the veterinary inspection, he really stands up and strides out in the trot-up – that is because he is absolutely scared stiff, it's hyper-alertness. People think 'Oh, he's so beautiful...', but all William wants to do is get out of there fast! He is getting better. He used to be very funny wherever there was a group of people together – he would spook at them or at a strange dog, or at some cows. That is just one of the problems with having a very clever horse. That cleverness can cause problems. In the dressage phase they can be too onward-bound or tense because they know they are going to gallop the next day, and so it is hard to get them calm and obedient enough. In the cross-country, those naturally bold horses often go through a phase of getting very cocky. They get a bit too big for their boots and hit problems when they start facing massive jumps because they have been too strong and brave. Then they seem to steady up and learn by their mistakes. By the time they are 10 to 14

years old, they are usually lovely because they have gone past all that and learnt from it. That is exactly what happened with both King William and Star Appeal. Both are instinctively very bold and went through a phase of getting very strong. At our first European Championship, William did this huge jump at a massive drop where all the other horses had been stopping, and he just collapsed at the bottom. It did him the world of good in a way, as it made him think that he did have to be a bit careful. Star Appeal got cocky and very strong, trying to run through the bridle, and he ran into a fence that he just didn't see. He didn't fall, but he hit it hard which gave him a surprise. Luckily, he was not hurt, and he came out of it much more careful and thinking about what he was doing. I just have to hope they will learn by their mistakes, because it is very easy to react by bitting them up too strongly.

You have got to keep calm and build up the trust over the years. If you watch horse and rider combinations, some riders seem to get all their horses going in a similar way. Some always seem to have horses that are a bit scatty, whereas others are always relaxed and laid-back – it is obviously the way that rider has produced their horses. So, if you can be calm as a rider, then, hopefully, it will have that effect on the horse. You must gradually build up, not doing too much with a young horse and over-facing it, and so blowing a lot of the trust you have started to build.

Look at top riders, like Mark Todd, and see how quiet he is as a rider, how still he is. He

'It is very important not to get cross with young horses...often they do not know what is right'

lets the horse get on and think for himself, leaving him alone as much as possible when galloping across country, as long as the horse is going forward and approaching each fence at the correct speed. You see some riders coming into the fence pulling and kicking. In that situation, the horse is half thinking about the rider and has only half his mind on the fence. Whereas the more free you can be as a rider, the more settled and focused the horse can be. Another example is Andrew Nicholson. Both the rounds he did at Burghley in 1995 were absolute classics. Neither of those horses are really good horses, but Andrew is a real master. He set off across country with them, his hands low, his reins fairly loose, and got them going. Both horses made mistakes in the first section of the course and poked a bit or left a leg on a few fences, but Andrew just sat there quietly, making sure they were going forward enough so they did not end up stopping. He let the horses work it out rather than trying to dominate them. With both horses it was simply fascinating to watch how they just grew and grew in confidence as they went around, because they were allowed to work it out for themselves.

I have a pretty special relationship with William. He is so talented across country he has always been brilliant, even as a young horse. From my very first event with him, he was straight and forward and jumped cleanly. We always clicked. Now he has settled, he is a very easy horse to ride cross-country and he absolutely loves it. You feel it is a real honour to ride a horse that is so talented and so enjoys it. Every time you come over a jump he is looking for the next fence, or, going round a corner, he is working out what is coming up next, so you just sit there! William and I know each other inside-

out now. He knows exactly how I think, and I know how he thinks. We totally understand each other. We try and give our horses as happy a life at home as possible, turning them all out for an hour or two every day so they get their freedom, and by varying their work. We have a lot of hills in our locality so we can do different things each day and keep their minds active. When we are preparing for the next event season, we get them out and about to competitions

"King William and I know each other inside out now. He knows exactly how I think, and I know how he thinks. We totally understand each other."

"This sport demands everything from a horse. I enjoy training the horses, starting off with a green, young horse who has no idea at all and building him up to that top level where he trusts you completely."

so they are kept interested and learning.

When it comes to training a young horse, you must always remember when you start working with him that he is totally ignorant. The horse does not know what life is about, or what he is meant to be doing. It is very important not to get cross with young horses. You see instances of riders getting after a horse because he has made a mistake, and often the poor horse doesn't know what is supposed to be right. So, if I was working for the dressage, for example, and the horse chucked his head in the air going from trot to canter, instead of telling him off, I would to try to explain that he must canter with his head down. I would move the horse around a little and try again. If the horse gets it right, he would get a pat, keeping very relaxed, so he knows that he has done what you wanted. On the other hand, if the horse does something wrong, you must immediately pick up on it. It is no good thinking 'Oh, that's all right', because the next time the horse will do it even more, because you didn't explain that was not what you wanted.

There is no point in the rider getting cross. You must make it clear – black and white – showing what is wrong and what is right. Obviously, if a horse starts taking advantage of a situation he must be reprimanded, but he must be rewarded at the right time, too. In this way he will learn more easily, and will be clear in his own mind as to what he meant to be doing. This is where the rider needs to be sensitive to what the horse is thinking and feeling. You cannot ride every horse the same, and you certainly cannot just dominate them all. When a horse is confident and competent at the level he's working at, then I know he is ready to go on and do more. If he feels bold and brave, if he is enjoying the work and you feel he has done enough at one level and is totally established there, then it is time to ask for a bit more. Often a rider has to be prepared to be creative in their approach to particular training difficulties, to increase a horse's enjoyment or motivation for the phase that is his weakest or which he finds most problematic. When I bought Boris he was quite stuffy and could not gallop very well. He had been a show horse and was round, soft and fat and didn't have a clue. What changed him totally was going hunting. He suddenly learnt that life could be terribly exciting, and he learnt how to gallop by galloping with the other horses, watching and copying them so he could really open up a stride and enjoy his speed. That was what worked, rather than persisting at home trying somehow to teach him how to gallop.

But sometimes it is teaching, and improving technique, that can help avoid problems before they happen. Often you can get to Intermediate level and then the ditches start getting really big and wide, and the horse gets scared of them. So I like to try and teach the horse from the start to take the ditches slowly on a loose rein rather than galloping at them. Horses can jump quite a big ditch from trot if you sit still, trot forwards and, if necessary, use another horse as a lead at first. The youngster has a natural instinct to copy and, going with an experienced horse, he will relax. In that way, he will learn to do it himself without always having to be urged.

The more talented a horse is at something, the easier it is for them to enjoy it and it is important that they do. In dressage, for example, if you are always having to ask them and if their ears are not forwards, it threatens the whole picture. King William least enjoys his showjumping because of the question of the tension and atmosphere, but

we have been working on this in several ways, mainly trying to get him into that kind of situation as much as possible so he learns how to cope with it. When I go to lecture-demonstrations we always take him so he gets used to the crowds and the clapping. It is all about getting a horse confident and believing in himself – not so that you are getting after him all the time – but building his own confidence and saying 'Yes, you can do it.'

My trainer, Lars Sederholm, is brilliant at working out what the horse is thinking, whether he is being lazy, or whether he is lacking confidence and is knocking a fence down because he feels he can't do it. If that is the case, we do exercises to improve the horse's style so he can do it, and then he is willing to give more because he starts believing in himself. You can soon demoralise a horse by making him feel he is useless. When a resistance problem comes up, you need to work out, as a rider, whether you think the horse is purely being naughty – in which case sort him out – or if he is lacking confidence and worried about a situation – when you obviously need a totally different approach. Then you have to build right up again, for example, putting the fence right down to help the horse regain the lost confidence that has made him resist.

In some ways, an event horse is a failure – he is not a good enough jumper to be a showjumper, doesn't move well enough to be a pure dressage horse, and he is not fast enough for racing. But the sport demands everything from a horse that he is capable of doing. I enjoy training the horses, starting off with a green, young horse who has no idea at all, and building him up to that top level where he trusts you completely. It's all about getting that partnership of absolute trust and understanding. **,**

MOTIVATION: THE PLUS FACTOR

When learning is easy, learning is fun – everyone thinks positive, confidence fills the air, the teacher is looked on as a helper and a friend. The pupil is in a state of high responsiveness – he is motivated to learn. When learning corresponds with hard work and complying with unappealing demands, then it is a chore. The teacher becomes 'the enemy'. The negative attitude becomes a handicap from the outset and leads to a downward spiral of demotivation.

In the wild the horse is motivated to perform its natural drives to eat, breed, move and socialise by its gene make-up, which in turn has been shaped by survival needs. The process is permanent, long-lasting and completely natural to it. Training for riding, and the other things we do with horses, is not natural and there is no inherent motivation to do it. But motivation in the short-term can be engendered if the trainer can make the learning process so pleasurable that it can be absorbed by the horse rather than impressed upon it. Good timing, effective two-way communication, going with the horse's own inclinations and showing him that it feels good when he does it right is all part of creating this atmosphere. But in what other ways can we make learning enjoyable and easy, increasing motivation rather than inadvertently demotivating the horse? Given consistently and continuously, rewards and praise act as general motivating influences as well as momentary enticements, because they foster a sense of achievement. Praise for a task well done is perhaps as effective in building up an atmosphere of co-operation and confidence as it is in providing an instant reinforcement for a particular response. It must be maintained though, whatever level the horse has reached, and always given whenever it is deserved.

Xenophon writes: "The gods have bestowed upon man the gift of teaching his brother man what he ought to do by word of mouth; but it is evident that by word of mouth you can teach a horse nothing. If, however, you reward him with kindness after he has done as you wish, he will be most likely to learn to obey as he ought. This rule...holds good in every branch of the art of horsemanship. For instance, he would receive the bit more readily if some good should come of it every time he received it; and he will leap and jump up and obey in all the rest if he looks forward to a season of rest on finishing what he has been directed to do." Consistency and clarity of communication gives the horse the sense of security it needs in order to be relaxed and ready to learn. If the rider can avoid giving muddled signals there should be no demotivating confusion. However much he wants to please, a muddled horse cannot work out what is required to make his rider pleased. What the rider needs is to be able to break a task down into steps the horse feels safe about and can deal with. The conversation has, as far as possible, to progress clearly and rationally one step at a time using the three Rs: Request, Response, Reward. Once the correct response has been given, a request must always stop, because continuing to nag away is totally confusing

'A muddled horse cannot work out what is required to make his rider pleased'

and only turns complying with the request into a punishment in itself. The riding school pony whose sides are numb from kicking has long since decided there is no point taking much notice, because when he goes forward he still gets kicked! If there is an objection to a request, we need to think why and, where necessary, increase the motivation to make a task a more attractive proposition. Where rules are required, as in the need for good manners, discipline needs to be consistent and immediate, such as the horse would receive in nature, because he appreciates knowing precisely where the goalposts are.

Variety is crucial to training at whatever stage the horse has reached. Though repetition is necessary for lessons to be logged into the memory, boredom invites resistances and the habituation principle guarantees that too much practice, especially without the motivation of reward, desensitises response. All horses perform better for variety within their work, whether it is the school hack or an advanced competition specialist. Minds crave stimulation and challenge, all the more so as they become increasingly agile and sensitive with learning. The comfortable security of 'follow my leader' or the same old familiar routine does not foster initiative or responsiveness – this applies to both horses and their riders.

TEMPERAMENT AND TALENT-SPOTTING

A cob is never going to make a great polo pony and a Thoroughbred is not the equine world's powerhouse, nor can we expect him to be. Horses have been selectively bred over centuries for the physique and attitude to suit particular jobs of work and, more recently, for specialist athletic and mental aptitudes. If a horse is not built to do a task that is set him, with the best will in the world he is going to find it difficult to oblige. Temperamental suitability is equally significant. As a general rule, most horses seem to enjoy activities that suit Equus' free-roaming, sociable nature – hacking, hunting, long distance rides, even racing (though not all are speedy enough to be first past the post). Less naturally enjoyable activities are potentially going to be more of an uphill struggle – school exercises, even jumping, are things that a wild horse would not need to apply his mind to or see any gain in wasting energy on.

When it comes again to specialisation, individual psychology becomes even more significant. Every owner or rider knows that horses have personalities, but what makes up this individuality? The personality is a particular individual's tendency to act in a certain consistent way at certain times. It is the product of a combination of inherited factors (breeding) and past experiences. These two influences interact to shape an individual horse's attitude to life in general, and also to particular situations. It could be said to be personality which produces the differences in horses which have had the same basic learning experiences.

Confidence or the lack of it, sensitivity and excitability do seem to be largely inherited personality traits. Training schedules should always have flexibility to allow for individual strengths and weaknesses. Some breeds and individuals, for example, are more easily distracted than others because they are more reactive and so require greater motivation to keep their attention on-task. These characters are more likely to get upset and confused if we make a mistake than more insensitive types. All horses respond to clear leadership, but it is the timid ones who suffer most in indecisive hands. If the dominant personality finds himself with the ditherer, it is the owner who is going to suffer! So matching rider with horse is important too.

The 'right' personality, or temperament, for a particular sphere of activity – creating a horse who is 'good at' what he does – is the one which is well adapted to that activity's environment. What suits one might be totally wrong in another. The shy, cautious soul will not make an event horse, but he will look after a novice rider in the way a self-confident, independent character could never be relied on to. The 'worrier' will thrive better in a stable, one-owner situation than in a busy teaching yard, or thrown into a competitive career involving ever-changing surroundings. That cocky individual, full of his own importance, is unlikely to be a good enough listener to make a Grand Prix dressage horse, or tolerant enough of mistakes to fit in at a riding school, but he has guts and loves a challenge. Across country he will jump his heart out for you. Though it will always be a case of horses for courses, with a sound basic education every horse can enjoy something and so become good at it, even if the goal is not competitive. Each will reach a certain level at which they are at their happiest and most comfortable – not all can be performance superstars. The trainer's task is to discover what a particular horse feels is pleasurable, rewarding and worth doing. Then, having discovered a talent, it is all about building on it. Nothing is more soul-destroying for a horse and rider than hammering away at a

job in which the horse, though it might get by, is never going to get that 'feel-good factor' that helps create a real partnership.

SUSIE HUTCHISON'S VIEW
A universally popular and respected figure in American showjumping, Susie Hutchison has spent almost 30 years competing successfully on the US Grand Prix circuit. Named American Grand Prix Association Rider of the Year in 1992, Susie's current string of horses include Samsung Clover Mountain, Bugs Bunny and Samsung Woodstock, fourth in the 1993 World Cup Finals.

' I have looked at an awful lot of horses, and so I trust my gut reaction when I go into a stable. I like a horse that has a special air about it. He should be saying: 'Dammit, I'm good!' He should have a look in his eye that shows character. Both of my current top horses, Woodstock and Bugs Bunny, have this special, intelligent look. They really think they are good!

What I want is a horse that looks around and is interested in what is going on around it and seems happy with the world. If a horse has this look, about 90 per cent of the time he will be true to form. I like it to be careful too for showjumping, so when I am trying a horse I will tap him on the ankle lightly with a branch. If he picks his leg up quickly, he is naturally sensitive and will probably be quite careful. If he doesn't move at all, I will stay away because he's not careful. I even free jump six-month-old babies over light bamboo poles occasionally,

'Horses have their own personalities. A rider must take his time to get into the mind of his horse'

as you can see then if they have a natural instinct. I try to avoid those that look as though they have been mishandled. Humans create so many horse problems, and, sadly, it's very hard to undo what has been done to a horse in the past. Horses remember.

A really 'good' horse can do anything, because all good horses have similar temperaments. They have an air of greatness. They have big hearts and a lot of try. They give 110 per cent. Some good horses have a little bit of an attitude which you have to work through, but that's just part of their personality. A good horseman is willing to put up with a bit of an attitude – it can work for you. When Woodstock arrived in the States he was very nasty in the stable, turning his back to me and putting his ears back. I wanted to know why, so I asked the lady who had had him as a three-year-old what he was like then, and she said she used to put her arms round him and hug him all the time. So I often wonder what happened to make him act the way he does. Now I've gotten to know him I realise he's full of hot air. If you are new to him or timid at all, he turns round and acts like he may kick. The stable is his domain. He definitely has an attitude! But then he is very brave. He will gallop round a course at top speed and leave the fences up. I really love going fast – sometimes I am already winning a class, but I still go fast because Woody can really run, he's amazing.

Bugs Bunny is an interesting character. He loves people and he is very expressive, always looking to please me. His biggest fault is that he just hasn't had enough show experience. Even though he is eleven years old, I have to think of him as still being a bit green. He will get in the ring and be distracted by a waving flag and leave a pole down. So, with him, I have to accept some

mistakes – he needs more big class experience and more time.

A good horse is like a good human athlete. A well-prepared human will get an adrenalin rush which helps him perform

"I believe in rewards, It's just like training a dog – a well-trained horse is a happy horse. He needs to have respect for his rider. I correct mistakes immediately but I reward good behaviour immediately, too."
Susie Hutchison schooling the eight-year-old Holsteiner, America One.
Photo: Lesley Ward.

better, and it's the same with a horse. He will rise to the occasion. I'm sure a good showjumper knows he is good and enjoys competing. There has to be that bond between the horse and the rider – a love and a mutual respect, an appreciation for each other. To be honest, when I am not at home I would rather have the horses exercised on a treadmill or a walker or lunged than have someone else ride them. If there is something wrong with a horse, I want to be the one to figure out how to work through the problem.

It is crucial to match a rider to a horse correctly. It's a great mistake to take a hot, sensitive horse and put a gung-ho, enthusiastic kid on it. Paul Shockemohle is a genius in putting horses and riders together. He would rather not sell the horse than sell a really careful horse to an inexperienced rider. If a horse is not going well, it is usually the rider's fault. Sometimes I have to sell a horse because he doesn't suit me. Even though I may love him, I may not be physically strong enough to ride him.

Once you can see that a horse has natural instincts, a good foundation of correct flatwork is very important. In my opinion, jumping is simply an extension of flatwork – the jumping is secondary. My top horses only jump at shows. Because they do flatwork all the time at home, jumping is fun for them. Occasionally the horses will go in the jumping chute without a rider, or before I jump a horse for the first time I may let him jump free in the chute. Then I can spot where he is most comfortable leaving the ground in front of a fence. Does he jump

short or take off long? This helps because you can help him take off where he does it best. Free jumping also teaches a horse better depth perception.

I only school a horse for around thirty minutes, working on shoulder-ins, half-passes, pirouettes and western roll-backs and spins at a high rate of speed. I practise galloping as fast as the horse can for short distances, so when the horse gets in the competition arena and we have to go fast in a jump-off, it's nothing new to him. The horse has learned to maintain his balance at higher speeds. All of my horses learn how to move at speed back at home. Sometimes I 'polo' my horse around like a barrel racer, using the jumps in the arena as barrels and going round them at the canter. You watch the western barrel racers – the riders usually gallop along at high speeds on a loose rein, and when they get to the barrel they take a contact and circle. That is what I am working towards. Western moves and training practices could really help a lot of English-style riders, as they keep a horse so nimble.

> **'You should ride because you love horses. The horse is the whole point'**

Lengthening and shortening the stride is also something I work on a lot, but first you need to establish a rhythm with the horse. Once you can maintain regularity at the walk, trot and canter, then you can play with his stride as you need. I work a lot on adjusting my horse's speed because I want them to be able to speed up and slow down when I tell them, as this is important in showjumping, and horses learn by repetition.

I don't like a horse to get bored. My coach, the late Jimmy Williams, taught the horses

"Horses are just like people, they have their own personalities. A rider must take time to get into the mind of the horse."
Photo: Lesley Ward.

tricks like putting their heads down on the ground, rolling balls around and stepping up on to a mounting block. I always want to keep a horse's mind active. If a horse feels lethargic and doesn't want to move forwards, we will go out on a trail or have a gallop round a field. What I want is a horse that is able to think for himself. A good showjumper must be clever and, even though he must think for himself, he must still listen to directions and be obedient.

I also believe in rewards, and I always carry sugar-cubes with me when I ride. I don't let a horse push me around for a treat though. It is just like training a dog – a well-trained horse is a happy horse. He needs to have respect for his rider. I correct mistakes immediately, but I reward good behaviour immediately too.

Sometimes we have a vision of how we want a horse to go, but we may have to change our methods. For instance, there were a couple of horses I was not having much success with. Even though Jimmy was a firm believer in maintaining rein contact to the jumps, he told me to throw their faces

171

away and let go completely in front of the jump, and they started going beautifully. It was totally contradictory to our way of teaching, riding and schooling, but it worked for those horses because we were open to a new way of doing things with them. So don't get too set in your ways. Woodstock, for example, had a rotten temperament. He had temper tantrums and was moody, but I have learned never to get mad with him. If you pick a fight with a horse, you will always lose because you're fighting out of your weight division!

Horses are just like people, they have their own personalities. A rider must take his time to get into the mind of his horse. I was taught to train a horse, not to just get on and ride, but to become mentally one with the horse. People say horses are dumb, but they outsmart us every day! Horses are our teachers and can teach us the right and wrong things to do. Every horse can teach you something new. The students we have start right off riding young green horses

with knowledgeable supervision; when they get a little better than the horse, they can go up in quality. It is not difficult to make a good horse good – it is difficult to keep him good. I was taught that it is what you learn after you think you know it all, that counts.

Horses have taught me to be more accepting and sensitive to the feelings of people. They are very humbling. I was fourth in the World Cup Finals, and then a week later I was riding in a show in California, and I fell off in front of everyone in the schooling arena – the horse jumped strangely and next thing I knew I was on the ground. I have also learned that winning is not everything. When you come out of the ring, if you are pleased with the way you rode and how your horse went for his level, that is the only thing that matters. You should ride because you love horses. The horse is the whole point. If you love winning ribbons more than you love the horse, you have lost sight of what is important.

,